THE BUSINESS OF FAUX

PATRICK GANINO

with ALLETAH GANINO

EAST
CAMBRIDGE
PRESS

D1450947

THE BUSINESS OF FAUX

</p>

First Edition

ISBN: 978 0-9778967-1-4

Published by East Cambridge Press
249 North Larch Street, Anaheim, CA 92805
info@eastcambridgepress.com
Distributed in the USA by Pathway Book Service:
Quantity Discounts available
pbs@pathwaybook.com

Photography: Mark Pogocsky and Vince Scarkno
Cover Design: Sherry Sparks
Quote: Anita Mediana
Graphic Production: Vicky Nuttall

Printed in the United States of America

Contents

Dedicated to...

...My wife Alletah, my three kids, Lauren, Carter, and Colson, my parents Bob and Eliza, and my sister Kate, without whom I would not have been able to do what I do. Special thanks to everyone who has helped me throughout my journey and to my Faux Forum family, which has brought a new inspiration into my life.

...And to Michael Sundell, whose efforts are not overlooked.

Chapter 1

Biography for Creative Evolution

My name is Patrick Ganino, and for the past ten years I've been the owner of a decorative painting business called Creative Evolution. During the process of growing a business from scratch, I've learned many things, often through trial and error, sometimes by accident. One thing I've learned, and that I firmly believe in, is that sharing knowledge and helping others always comes back to you in the long run. I've also come to the realization that the world is full of talented artists as well as talented businessmen and women. Unfortunately, the two rarely go hand-in-hand, so I decided to write this book in order to share my business strategies with other faux and mural artists. It is my hope that this book will help you bring your decorative painting business to its full potential.

You might be asking yourself, "What makes this guy qualified to give other people advice?" That's a good question, and if you're hoping I have a PhD in business or even took some night courses along the way, you're in for a disappointment. I learned everything I know about business, and most of what I know about decorative painting, the old-fashioned way—through hard work, experience, creativity, determination, and many, many mistakes.

My story actually begins about 25 years ago, when I was a little kid of 7 years, hoping to score some quick cash. I set up a lemonade stand, made a few bucks, and from that point on devoted much of my time and energy to making money. In the seventh grade, I came up with a system of making t-shirts to sell to my classmates. I bought a bunch of plain shirts, created my own designs, transferred them to the shirts, and sold them around school. Small stuff, of course, but this trend of coming up with my own ways of making money started early and has lasted my whole life.

At the age of 15, my best friend and I took a job that probably did more to teach me about approaching people and selling them on an idea than anything else I've done. We went door to door, selling tri-fold books of coupons for local restaurants. Each book cost twenty dollars and could be used ten times to buy one meal and get one free. My friend and I kept 50% of the money made from the books, so here we were running around, making one, sometimes two, hundred dollars a night. It gave me a really good idea of how to get people's guards down, which I think is something that can be learned with a little bit of effort and some common sense. Here's an example of how we worked. One evening my friend and I walked up to a home in order to sell some coupon books. In the front yard we saw a woman watering her flowers. We started in with our sales pitch, though it was obvious she wasn't interested. She said, "Look, I'm watering my flowers right now. I don't have any money on me."

Of course this was just a polite excuse, but that didn't mean we had to accept it and walk away! I casually took the hose from her and started watering the plants myself. I said, "Don't worry, I'll take care of the plants while you grab your checkbook." At this point I guess she could have grabbed the hose back and sprayed us with it so we'd leave her alone, but she didn't. Instead, she went inside and got the checkbook. She made out a check while I watered the flowers. Simply by loosening her guard and being a little persistent, we made some money.

I graduated high school and, at the age of 18, moved to Florida. I briefly went to art school, but it wasn't for me. College had never been my top priority, but under family pressure and lack of a better direction for myself, I chose a school in Florida. My reasons for attending this particular school were completely shallow. I had friends there and Florida seemed like a great place to live. After briefly suffering through classes centered around, for example, drawing couches, I made the decision to drop out. I'd always enjoyed art and showed talent, but hadn't considered making it a career. For a while I had a job as a valet, which led me to start my own valet service. This taught me how to organize and earn short-term cash. I also got to drive some pretty awesome cars! Then, I ended up doing a mural for a nightclub and made an astounding five hundred dollars. That was a lot of money to me then, so I eagerly took a job painting another nightclub mural, which led to a mural in a restaurant. I met an artist who specialized in gold leafing and distressing. He took me on as an apprentice, and from that point on I knew what I wanted to do. Unfortunately, I didn't know **how** to do it from a business standpoint.

Being somewhat directionless at that point, I moved back to Connecticut where I later met my wife, Alli. We were both working in typical 9 to 5 office jobs, and I hated it. Having a boss looking over my shoulder all the time, doing the same thing day in and day out, drove me crazy. But I was getting married and needed a steady income, something predictable and stable. While we were planning our wedding reception, Alli and I went to a very nice local restaurant to talk to the manager about possibly having the event there.

As we talked about the wedding, the manager mentioned that they were in the process of adding a VIP room but were having trouble finding someone who could paint a mural for them and stay within budget. I don't even know what made me say it, since it had been a while since I'd done a mural and I wasn't all that experienced to begin with. My mouth just popped open and I said, "I can do it." Next thing you know, I'm not only married, but painting a large mural for the first time in years and, to top it all off, Alli and I are expecting our first child.

Fast forward several months. I'm still plugging away at my office job and pretty much hating it. Alli and I are the proud parents of a beautiful little girl. To my surprise, I've gotten several phone calls from the owner of the restaurant where I painted the VIP room mural. Customers have been asking for my name, and the owner wants to know if I have some business cards I can drop off for him to hand out. All along I thought there wasn't a strong enough demand for decorative painting to support myself on, let alone a growing family. At that time, in the late 1990's, faux was just creeping into the state. The "old money" preferred wallpaper and HGTV hadn't really begun yet to fuel the faux finish flames. After the response I got to that initial restaurant mural though, I started to rethink the market for decorative painting. Alli and I talked it over, and she urged me to take a chance and try running my own business. The next day I went into work, handed in my resignation, and never looked back.

The first year really tested our resolve, since we were basically living on one income, but we made it. One small thing that made a big difference for me personally was a small card I made to carry in my wallet. I still have the card to this day—just a plain index card with these words written on it: "Be hard. Be smart. Patience, pride, control, energy, motivation, love, money." Whenever I started to feel my focus slipping, I took the card out of my wallet and read it to myself. I needed the inspiration and reaffirmation from those words.

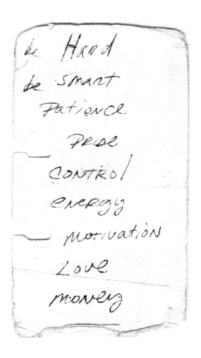

My total income that year, before taxes, was $15,000. The next year it doubled. Then, in my third year of business, I faced my biggest challenge yet. One morning on the way to a job, I was in a car accident. It's the kind of thing you never expect, and are never truly prepared for. The accident left me with some minor injuries as well as a broken vertebra in my back. For six weeks I couldn't work at all, had no disability insurance, no income coming in, and a family to support.

At the time my daughter was about two and a half years old, and my wife had changed jobs to be closer to home and spend more time with the family. What this really meant was that she was making less money than when I first began my business and her income alone wasn't enough to support us for long. The combination of enforced bed rest, worry about finances, and stress over my business fueled an anger in me that I hadn't thought possible. For the first time, I realized that I had a job, not a business. I began looking for someone to train as a faux finisher, not only to help cover situations when I was unable to work, but to also bring in passive income.

I knew that if I could pay someone to do faux finishes while I painted murals, I had the potential to bring in more money for my business which would give me the ability to expand into other avenues. Recovering from the car accident was one of the worst times in my life, and yet it led to so many positive things. From that point on, income from the business continued to grow quickly.

Once we had a nice little cash flow coming in, I took that money and put it back into the business. Almost ten years later I have a thriving faux and mural business, a decorative painting school, a series of how-to DVDs in production, and four websites devoted to different aspects of the decorative painting field. It's been quite a ride, and I'd like to share with you what I've learned about growing a successful decorative painting business.

To learn more about faux and share with other artists,

join us at the FauxForum.

Chapter 2

Marketing

Taking the first steps toward building your own business and realizing your dreams can be an intimidating and overwhelming venture. With the right tools and knowledge, however, the journey can be immensely rewarding on many levels. I've talked to artists from all over the country, and the one thing many of them are missing is a solid business sense. It's also important to have some basic people skills, since what you're really doing is selling yourself and selling your work. However, before you can sell anything you have to market yourself. No one is going to buy something from you if they don't know you're out there. I have a very close friend who makes up for any lack of experience or business know-how with an endless supply of determination and energy. Learning from mistakes and having the temerity to try again, and again, and again, until you hit on something that works for you will make your success where others have failed. Throughout this process, keep in mind that energy and positive thinking can make all the difference in the world, especially when paired with creativity. I've tried many different marketing techniques, some great and others not so great. Of course I'll only discuss here the marketing strategies that paid off for me, and touch briefly on some things that didn't pan out.

Business Cards

Before you do anything else, have some business cards printed up. They don't need to be elaborate or expensive, but they do need to convey clearly who you are and what you do. If you can include a picture of your work on the card, definitely do that. The card should also include your business name, your name, a concise description of the services you offer, and all of your contact information. The main contact phone number for your clients should be your cell phone. The reason for this is even if you move to a new town or switch service providers, your cell phone number can stay the same. You can save yourself a lot of trouble not having to reprint business cards. Give people options for contacting you and try to be constantly available. In addition to your cell phone number, include a second phone number (probably your home or office number), and your email address. If someone can't get in touch with you, they're going to call the next name on their list and you might miss out on a good lead. There's nothing worse than losing a job simply because clients can't find you.

Portfolio

A professional portfolio of your work is essential. I cannot stress enough how much of an impression your portfolio makes on the client. For that reason, one of the first things you need to do is create a portfolio that not only looks professional but show-cases your abilities and strengths. You may ask, "How can I have such an amazing tool when I'm just starting out?" There are some simple ways to build a high-quality portfolio even if your professional experience is limited.

Digital Cameras

First, I would highly recommend buying a digital camera if you don't already have one. It doesn't need to be top-of-the line with all the bells and whistles, but it should have plenty of memory, a large enough view screen for you to tell if you've taken a good shot, zoom, decent resolution, and a minimum of 6 megapixels. My digital camera cost $200 and has everything I need to take good pictures for my portfolio. Compared to the cost of hiring a photographer to take pictures of your work, the one-time investment of a digital camera is a true bargain.

If you don't have photos of work you've done, go back and take pictures. Take several shots from many different angles. If you have a digital camera you can delete or simply not develop the pictures you aren't happy with. Most clients, in my experience, are happy to arrange for you to take photos of your work even well after the job has been completed. You can also retake photos if you aren't happy with any you might already have, or if you feel they don't do your work justice. If you need some guidance in taking photos, look in a home décor magazine to see how they set up their shots, then try to mimic them.

Another way to fill out your portfolio is to photograph sample boards. Create a variety of large sample boards using different colors and finishes. Place each board on top of a table, propped against the wall and photograph it. Obviously, the board should fill up the image so it doesn't look like a picture of a sample board. To add a nice flair, place a vase of flowers or some other nice decorative object in front of the board. The finished photo will look like a close-up shot of a wall in a client's home. This is not "cheating" if you did the finish and can recreate in someone's home. I still have a few photos done this way in my portfolio, because they do look very nice. If you decide to use photos of sample boards in your portfolio, make sure you place a different object in front of the sample for each picture. Your goal is to have a professional portfolio, not to have to admit to a client that each photo has the same vase of flowers because you painted boards, not other people's homes!

You can also paint your own home, your parents' home, your friend's home, anything, to gain experience as well as photos for your portfolio. Technically you only need to paint one wall to have a photograph for your portfolio, but keep in mind that painting the entire room gives you more options for good pictures. Actually doing the work in someone's home also lets you work out the kinks in a job beforehand. If you're new to Venetian plaster, for example, you'd certainly want to practice on more than a sample board before you step into a client's home with plaster and trowel in hand. It's much better to make mistakes in your own dining room, or your best friend's, than a paying customer's. When the room is finished, you not only have some great new photos for your portfolio, but more experience under your belt.

Once you've taken the photos, have them developed. The pictures should all be the same size. I feel that 8 X 10 works best for showing detail, texture, color variations, etc. If you have quality photos of good work, you certainly don't need to buy an expensive portfolio. A simple three-ring binder with plastic sleeves for your photographs will do nicely. Create a separate section in the portfolio for each type of work you offer, for example, Murals, Faux Finishes, Children's Rooms. If you feel the need for a more professional appearance with your portfolio, you can have a hardbound book made featuring your work. Most online digital photo processing companies offer these books, usually referred to as memory books. The website I use is www.snapfish.com. You can upload your photos, choose the order and size of photographs in your book, and write a caption for each picture. These books are relatively inexpensive, about $20.00 for a 20 page book. If you order a few copies of this type of portfolio, you can give the extras to decorators you work with so they can share them with their own clients.

In addition to your portfolio of photographs, it's a good idea to have a portfolio of sample boards in a variety of finishes and colors. I use styrene boards, which are large, light, and flexible. I carry them in a large artist's portfolio case—it basically looks like a big, flat suitcase. There are a couple of good reasons to carry sample boards like this to a meeting. One, you can hold the board up to a wall in order for a client to visualize how a particular color or finish will look in their home. Two, many distinctive finishes have a wonderful texture and movement that isn't always easy to capture in a photograph. I encourage clients to feel the texture of a plaster or glazed board, turn it to see the way light plays off the surface, or notice how a raised stencil adds depth. These can be wonderful selling points, especially for high-end finishes, that photos simply can't convey on their own. Try to avoid overwhelming a client with too many samples, however. Having ten to twelve sample boards along with your portfolio of photographs gives a client a strong impression of your skills and a good sense of your level of professionalism.

Paint Stores

Once you have business cards, start visiting all of the paint stores in the area. A good paint store can be your best friend. Stop in, introduce yourself to the owner or manager, explain what you do, and leave a stack of cards. I feel that paint stores are a very important asset because they have the ability to refer you to customers who come in asking about decorative painting services. You can help further your own cause by making sure the store managers or owners know they'll be getting your business if they refer you to their customers. You are also doing them a favor by patronizing their store. This is a symbiotic relationship where they need you as much as you need them.

When I first started out, I went to many, many paint stores because at that point I had no loyalty to one store in particular. The more business I did, the more I found I liked some stores and wasn't that crazy about others. Keep in mind that you and the paint store have different goals. The store wants to sell product quickly and efficiently. You need more specialized services, such as matching colors or mixing custom colors. These things take more time from store employees, and you may need to shop around before you find a place that's willing to go above and beyond for you. Once you do, stick with that store and give them as much of your business as is practical. They'll repay you with referrals and be one of your most valuable resources. I've been using one paint store for the vast majority of my supplies for several years now, and they've not only given me storage space for paint, but referred me to some fantastic clients. One lead they gave me in my second year in business was for the renovation of the Wadsworth Mansion in Middletown, CT. The designer for the project came into the paint store and was referred to me. She called me, I got the job, and made $8,000.00 from it. At the time it was the largest commission I'd ever seen. Along with that, they referred countless smaller jobs to me. Those jobs got me through the start of my business and allowed me to bring in more income so I could continue growing and expanding.

Fliers

Creating and distributing your own fliers is another low-cost marketing strategy that can work well when you are first starting out. The fliers don't have to be elaborate or professionally made. All you need to do is use a simple computer program such as Paint or Adobe to design your fliers, then have color copies made at a local print shop. The cool thing about fliers is that they are a visual way to attract customers to a visual industry. Make your fliers eye-catching, include all pertinent contact information, and hang them up in any public place with a bulletin board. Your flyer will stand out from the papers advertising labradoodle puppies or trumpet lessons simply because it is unique. Be reasonable in your expectations from the fliers—most of the calls you get will be for small jobs. Remember though that money is money, and you have to start building a client base and reputation somewhere. Even a modest client or a small job can, and will, lead to more impressive and lucrative work.

When hanging fliers, be creative about where you put them. Feel free to go into a large office building and ask the receptionist at the desk if you can hang a flier in the break room or cafeteria. You have nothing to lose by asking, and can reach a broad range of people in this way. Early on in my business I hung a flyer in the break room at a large office building. That flyer, which cost me only pennies to make, led to some work for a client who I consider a "connector." Such clients have been a crucial element to my business. A connector is a person who loves getting other people together and will refer you to everyone they know. This client hired me to do some work in his home. He then talked about my business to literally everyone he knew, which led to more and more work for me. At one point I added up my income from all of the work that originated with his referrals and the total was about a hundred thousand dollars. It's amazing if you think about it—that one job in his home led to so many other opportunities, simply because he was a connector. All of that from one little flier that basically cost me nothing except a little bit of effort. I joke in our business class as I hold up a copy of that flier, "This sheet of paper is worth $100,000." It certainly gets them thinking!

Cold Calls

Don't be afraid of the phone. When you first start your business you've got a lot of time to kill because you don't have much work. Take a break from making sample boards to spend an hour a day on the phone. Haul out the phone book or go online and look up architects, designers, contractors, painting companies, and paint stores. Tell them what you do and ask if they might be in need of your services. You're going to get turned down 90% of the time and you'll probably get discouraged, but keep at it. Follow up the phone calls with a letter restating what you do and be sure to include a business card. If you stick with it, you will land something. My first year in business I made so many phone calls, and most of them didn't pan out. However, I did talk to a contractor from southwestern CT who owned a company doing a lot of work in high-end homes. He gave me a lot of restoration work, small jobs that paid well. For example, I went into one home with an expensive wallpaper that had been discontinued. The wallpaper had been damaged in some places, and my job was to match the colors and hand paint the design back onto the wallpaper. At times it was tedious, but again, I was making money and working for people who passed on my name for bigger and better jobs. All it took on my part was time and effort, and it paid off.

So let's say you've been getting your name out and have gotten some work and now have a few dollars in your pocket. Your overhead should be really low and you should have some positive cash flow at this point. Instead of buying that great pair of boots you saw in the store the other day, put that money right back into your business. It's critical to always remember that your business will only be as good as you want it to be. It's kind of like raising a child. You provide them with the tools necessary to grow in life, putting their needs first and devoting yourself to helping them reach their potential. Your business needs to be nurtured in order to grow.

Newspaper Ads

One obvious and tempting form of marketing is the newspaper. Personally, I've never gone this route. I know other people who have spent the money for a large ad in the paper, and it doesn't seem to be worth the money from my perspective. I think there are better ways to put that money to good use. The possible exception to this rule is to go with a local, small-town paper. Don't go crazy and buy a full-page ad, but instead use a small blurb about who you are and what you do. If you go this route, you'll probably have more success. Keep in mind, however, that there are ways to have a newspaper promote you for free, which I'll talk about later.

Mail-outs

You might also be tempted to go to a nice neighborhood and stuff some mailboxes. It seems like a good idea, but it's against federal law. You have to actually stamp and mail your advertisements if you want to avoid prosecution, as I'm sure all of us do. There probably isn't a big market for decorative painting in prison unless you're a tattoo artist as well, so I'd suggest finding a service to provide you with names and addresses within your target market. The company I've used is called InfoUSA.com (www.infousa.com). It's really a very simple process. From their website, you fill out a form with specifications as far as what type of clientele you're looking for. You can narrow down the population of your area by age, income, house value, etc. What this gives you is a list of names and addresses that meet your standards. For a bit of extra money, you can even have this information sent to you on pre-printed labels.

When you fill out a form of this kind for a lead service, keep in mind the type of client you would like to have. Decorative painting is a luxury item, so confine your search to higher-than-average income brackets and house values. Aim your search at upper middle class homes and higher. In Connecticut, for example, I'd target homes valued at $450,000.00 and up. Depending on your geographical area, you'd need to modify that amount. Do some research online or check the real estate section of the paper to see how much homes are selling for and in what areas. This should give you a good idea of the clientele you want to reach. At the same time, avoid advertising yourself in this way to **only** the highest-income homes in your area. You want to reach people who can afford your services in general, not just the ones who can pay for an entire house full of custom finishes and murals. I can't stress enough how important it is to keep in mind that even a modest job can, and usually does, lead to bigger and better things.

Now that you have your list of potential clients, what do you send them? The key is to design a mail-out brochure that won't instantly be tossed into the garbage. An eye-catching postcard featuring one or two of your most impressive portfolio images, contact information, and a detailed list of services works well. Postage for postcards is also less expensive. If you invest in a good supply of postcards, you will find other uses for them down the road as well. A color brochure that can be folded and taped or sealed at one edge is also a good form of mail-out. It gives you more space to show off your work or describe the services you offer. Whichever form of mail-out you choose, be sure it is professional, concise, and visually interesting.

There are a couple of things to keep in mind when you get ready to send off your mail-outs. Timing is very important. If you send them out on December 20th, you're simply not going to catch anyone's attention. There's just too much going on that time of year. Instead, time your mail-outs for spring and fall, which is when most people start thinking of home improvements they'd like to do anyway. Aim for February, March, April, September, and October. It's also a good idea to include a return address on each mail-out. If any are sent back to you as undeliverable, you can take that address off of your list and not waste a future mail-out.

ve Evolution specializes in deco-
inting, faux finishes, Trompe
d custom murals including chil-
oms. Our work has been fea-
everal articles and can be seen in
ts and businesses, as well as pri-
ies.

feel free to browse through our
ortfolio to view examples of
the decorative work we have
d at www.creativeevolution.net

Patrick Ganino
Owner & Faux Designer

ww.creativeevolution.net

Murals:

Whether you envision a garden in your living room or a seascape in your bathroom, custom murals are the ideal way to individualize your home. If you can imagine it, I can paint it.

Children's Rooms:

From fairy tales to your child's favorite storybook characters, a special design for your child's room is a simple way to create an entire world for your child's imagination to grow in.

Faux Finish:

Faux finishes can add a dramatic or subtle touch to any room and can bring out your home's true potential. Finishes include sponging, ragging, dragging, color washes, stripes, and many, many more.

Trompe l'Oeil:

This decorative painting technique creates the illusion of depth to trick the eye into seeing a painting as a three-dimensional object. From moldings to shelves, trompe l'oeil adds a classic and intriguing look to your home.

Creative EVOLUTION

www.creativeevolution.net

EMAIL: sales@Creativeevolution.net
Info@Creativeevolution.net

As an alternative to paying for a list of customers, you can take a drive around a neighborhood you've recently worked in and write down the addresses. Your mail-outs could then announce that you've recently completed a custom decorative painting project in the neighborhood. As an extra incentive, consider offering a limited-time discount to new clients in that area. Or, take a drive in an area you'd like to target for new clients, write down addresses, and mail your information to them. This method requires more leg-work and time on your part but can be less expensive than purchasing the information from a service.

Home Shows

Once you get some extra money in your business account (not your pocket, because you're putting money back into the business remember?), you can invest some of it in a booth at a home show. Home shows are an unbelievable outlet to get instant business. As a sole proprietor, the only employee, I had a good amount of work and a comfortably long waiting list. When I decided to expand my business a little bit by subcontracting out much of the faux work, I suddenly found myself hustling to book enough clients to keep more than one person busy. However, a home show can also jump-start a business in its early stages or add to the clientele of even a seasoned artist.

Typically home shows are held in the spring and fall, usually in some kind of arena or civic center. The company sponsoring the home show rents floor space to businesses wishing to advertise at the show. Each business pays around a thousand dollars for approximately a ten by ten space on the floor. Rows of booths are separated by a curtain, and other than that, the space is empty. Your home show booth is yours to fill, and what you choose to put in that space will determine the success of your booth.

Home shows bring in a huge amount of people. In one weekend, it's normal for ten to twelve thousand prospective clients to walk past your business's space. That's a lot of people. If you set up your booth properly, you will do very well. I've seen many faux finishers and muralists advertise at home shows, and afterwards almost all of them complain about not doing very well. It all boils down to the set-up of their booth. If you've ever been to a home show, I'm sure you've seen companies who set up their booth and place a fishbowl on their table. Usually next to the fishbowl is a sign encouraging you to enter a contest to win some sort of fabulous prize, like a free hot tub or gutters that never need to be cleaned. Of course, what the company does with all of those entry forms is build a prospective customer list. You enter the contest, and then you get a phone call or brochure in the mail trying to sell you the product all over again. **This is the wrong way to do it!** In my mind, those leads are not legitimate because most people think they are signing up for a prize and really have no interest in the product being sold. You want legitimate leads, prospective clients who **do** want what you're offering.

In order to accomplish this, your booth must stand out from the others. Lucky for you, the nature of your business all but guarantees attention. To set up your home show space, you will need a table and chairs. Sometimes these can be rented from the home show company, but in my experience they charge so much that you may as well purchase them yourself, especially if you plan on doing more than one show. Cover the table with a nice tablecloth and place something pretty on it, such as a potted plant. For the floor of the booth, I have a nice area rug to give the space a more finished feel. As I said before, there are curtains behind the space to separate aisles. Use these curtains to show off your work. Choose several of your most impressive portfolio photos and have them blown up to poster sizes. Any print or copy shop can do this for you, and it isn't very expensive. Hang these posters on the curtains using hooks, which will provide a great backdrop for your booth. I suggest using photos of murals if possible simply because they tend to attract more attention. Once the mural shots have drawn people in, they'll be sold on the faux finishes in your portfolio. If you plan to focus on finishes and not offer murals, choose the most eye-catching finishes from your portfolio to display in your booth. Photos with a lot of color and movement, maybe featuring stenciled borders or patterns. I've also noticed that faux marble and woodgraining simply amaze people. Once you have a prospective client's attention, your portfolio will do most of the selling for you.

Now we come to the most important part of your home show booth. Along with that lovely potted plant on the table, set up a stack of business cards, detailed brochures, and at least one portfolio. I have two copies of my portfolio out on the table so strangers don't have to share and no one has to wait for a turn. Along with these things, you must have one crucial item—a sheet of paper inviting prospective clients to sign up for a free consultation or in-home estimate. This sign-up sheet is key. It doesn't have to be flashy or colorful. In fact, mine is a simple page with spaces

for name, address, phone number, and the best time to call. I've
noticed that no one likes to be first on the list, so add one or two
"fakes" at the top to break the ice. Don't forget to put a pen on
the table next to the sign-up sheet!

Once your booth is set up and looking fabulous, take a seat
behind the table and prepare to spend the day smiling. You don't
need to stand outside your booth and usher people in for a close
look at your portfolio, and certainly don't shout at passers-by
to stop and sign up. Let the photos behind you do the talking.
When people stop to take a look at the posters, invite them to go
through your portfolio. Answer questions if they have them, but
otherwise stay quiet. Follow their cues, and if they ask questions
or seem at all interested, hand them a business card and let them
know they can sign up for a free consultation. There's no need to
push or sell hard, just be friendly and confident.

After the show, once your facial muscles have relaxed from all
that smiling, get right to work on your list of prospective clients.
That piece of paper has everything on it you need to make the
home show a worthwhile investment of time and money. Choose
a good time of day to call, such as late evening when people are
usually finished with dinner but not yet in bed for the night. I
usually spend two or three evenings after a home show making all
of these calls. It is critical that you contact the people on your list
within a few days of the show. If you wait even two weeks, they'll
have lost interest and the leads will be completely cold.

What do you say when you make your phone calls? Start by
introducing yourself and remind the client why you are calling. I
usually say something like this: "Hello, this is Patrick Ganino of
Creative Evolution. I'm calling because you signed up for a free

decorative painting consultation at the home show on Saturday. Would you like to schedule a meeting?" Sometimes I have to repeat this and go into more detail about who I am and what I do before they remember me, and this is only a day or two later. Imagine if I waited a week! Not everyone on your list will actually meet with you. They may ask to get back to you when they are "ready." Don't be discouraged, just move on to the next call. Try to schedule meetings in the very near future, and be ready to work around the client's schedule. The majority of my meetings take place at the end of the day or on weekends when my customers aren't out working themselves.

Not all of the business you receive from the home show will happen right away. Many times, I'll get a call several months or even a year after a home show from someone who picked up my card. It's pretty common for new clients to wait until their renovations are almost complete before calling, or for someone building a new home to hold onto your card until they are ready for your services. That's one bonus about home shows—you build up your client base in both the short term and the long term. You can also count on referrals from clients who met you at a home show to keep the work coming in at a steady pace. I've found that doing one home show in the spring and one in the fall helps to fill out my work schedule very nicely, not just for myself but for the subcontractors I use as well.

Chapter 3

Preparing to Meet the Client

Now that you know how to attract clients, it's important to know how to handle your first meeting with a new client. You have a professional portfolio and the knowledge to complete the work, but you still need to sell yourself, and your work to some extent, to prospective clients.

Don't let a negative view of selling prevent you from being outgoing and open with your clients. "Selling" seems to have a negative connotation today. We tend to automatically think of a used car salesman, someone pushy and aggressive trying to con us out of hard-earned money. In reality, there's nothing wrong with being an honest salesperson. Selling is only negative when the product being sold doesn't meet expectations or live up to the seller's description. The majority of the world sells one thing or another, whether it's for a monetary exchange or not. We all "sell" every day; for example, stressing a viewpoint to a friend or explaining to someone why they might want to buy one brand of shoe instead of another. Instead of being shy about selling, focus on presenting yourself and your work in a positive light and live up to your own claims. Your product needs to back up your words if you want to keep your current clients happy and earn referrals to new clients.

When I first started my business, I went out of my way to look professional for meetings with clients. I wore nice pants, not jeans, a button-down shirt and tie, and good shoes. After a while I figured out that if I went to a meeting looking like a painter, no one was going to be surprised. I still keep a clean (i.e. paint-free) shirt in my car to throw on sometimes, but if my jeans and shoes have some paint on them, I don't worry about it anymore. I do still make sure my hair is combed and I don't look like a complete slob. No one has ever said to me, "Well, we like your work a lot, but there was too much paint on your shirt so we hired someone else. Sorry." Bottom line, your clothes can be paint-spattered, but if underneath that the customer can see you as an honest and straightforward person you'll be fine.

You can lose a client before you even meet face-to-face. Odds are you aren't the only decorative painter in your area, and if a new client has a hard time getting in touch with you, they're more likely to simply call someone else. So, make sure you're available to take calls whenever possible. You might choose to let calls go to voicemail during the day and then answer them in the evening, but be aware that you're taking a risk. Many people simply won't leave a message. Others might leave a message but will then call the next name on their list. I carry my cell phone everywhere and very rarely miss a call. Of course, I make an exception if I'm meeting with a client. When I'm in a meeting, I do not interrupt the client's time to take a call. When I do have a phone call to return, I make it a priority to do so as soon as I possibly can.

If you are going to be even five minutes late, call to let your clients know. It prevents the client from becoming annoyed with you, and it makes you look thoughtful. If you have to reschedule an appointment for any reason, do it as far in advance as you can. Don't wait until ten minutes before the meeting is supposed to take place. Obviously in the case of an emergency people can be very understanding, but in the course of everyday business, no one wants to feel as if they aren't a priority to you. I make it a point to be at least 15 minutes early for my appointments. It gives me a little bit of leeway if traffic is bad or some other unforeseeable event comes up. If I'm really early, I'll park a little ways down the street, catch up on some phone calls, or just listen to the radio. But I'm always on time.

The key to being a good salesman is to make it easy for someone to buy what you're selling. Have you never been in a situation where you wanted to buy something, but the person selling it was making it really hard? I once went to an electronics store to buy a wall mount for my TV. After telling three or four different people what kind of TV I had, what size it was, and the way I wanted it mounted on the wall, someone finally figured out which item I should buy. After all of this, they told me the item wasn't in stock and couldn't currently be ordered. I asked, "What about that one?" and pointed to the display model. The answer was, "Well, we don't have a box for that and we aren't supposed to sell the display…" There I was, with cash in hand, ready to buy something and putting a lot of effort into getting it, but had to walk away because the sellers were making things too difficult. Don't be that kind of seller. Take whatever money people are willing to give you, in whatever form they want to give it. Cash, of course. Personal checks, fine. Credit cards, yes. Accepting credit cards is very easy. The company I use is called Merchant Warehouse (www.merchantwarehouse.com). It's simple to set up and gives your clients another payment option. The fees for the service are reasonable, but of course I'd suggest researching all of your options before choosing a service that suits your needs.

Before you meet with a prospective client, there are certain papers you'll want to have in order. First, keep a copy of your business license and business insurance with you, possibly at the back of your portfolio. Not many customers will ask to see these things, but some will. Acquiring a business license is a must, and the process varies from state to state. Visit your state government's website, find out what the requirements are in your state, and do what you need to do for a license as soon as possible. The same goes for insurance. It is an absolute necessity. Look into different policies and choose one that works for you. I'd suggest having at least two million dollars in liability coverage.

Another important piece of paper you'll want to bring to a meeting is your contract. I've included here a copy of my contract as a basic reference, but keep in mind that laws vary from state to state. Contact a business lawyer or ask another decorative painter in your area (this is why it's good to have those contacts) to find out what your contract should or should not contain. The reason for using a contract is simple. The contract protects both you and the customer from misunderstandings or questions down the road. The contract states who the client is, what work will be done, how much you will be paid, and how changes to the work must be handled. This is important. Anything about a job that changes, including additions to the work, must be in writing. Adjust the price accordingly and have the client sign off on the new work order. The vast majority of your jobs will go smoothly with no one taking another look at the contract, but it is an important tool to have for those occasions with a misunderstanding about what the job included or the final price pops up. Having a detailed list of work to be performed also helps clear up the client's ideas of what exactly you will do. If you basecoat the room yourself and charge for it, the client needs to know that. The work order should state whether or not you will paint the trim. A lot of people will assume that painting the trim is included in the cost. If you've ever had the misfortune to paint trim, you know that it's not a given or a "freebie" thrown in with the job. Your client may not know this. So, before you start booking jobs, take the time to develop a solid contract. Besides protecting your interests and your client's interests, it will give you a more professional and credible appearance.

As far as the work order goes, you can create a simple form on the computer and print out multiple copies. Something with your business letterhead at the top works well. Once you and your client have decided on the details of the job, fill out the work order, have the client sign it, and keep a copy. This can be done at any point that's convenient for you before you start the job—at the initial meeting, when you have a follow-up meeting to show custom samples to a client, etc. When changes are made, you have the work order on file to refer to and adjust accordingly. I don't think you need to whip it out of your pocket if a client walks into the room and suggests adding a few more birds to a mural, but if the changes to the original job are significant enough to change the price, as soon as you can have the client sign off on things, do so.

In The Client's Home

When you walk into a client's home, the first thing they notice about you is your demeanor. Before they even see your portfolio, they're already deciding how they feel about you, probably on a subconscious level. It's important for you to go into a meeting with an air of confidence, a casual, laid-back type of attitude. If the client feels that you are honest and straightforward, not nervous or pushy, they're far more likely to write to a check before you walk out of their house.

I also firmly believe that the key to closing the deal is to walk the client through a series of events while letting them feel as if they are in control of the meeting. It's their house, their idea of how to decorate the house, and their money. The majority of your clients will be commissioning a mural or faux job for the first time. They might not be sure about what to expect, but at the same time won't respond well to you if you march into their house and rush them through the process. I can't begin to count how many times I've gone into a meeting and ended up staying much longer than expected just chatting, getting to know the clients, hearing about their kids and vacations. Your clients will want to get to know you a little bit as well in most cases, so don't brush aside the small talk. Avoid making the conversation all about yourself. I've had clients tell me they really enjoy speaking with me, although in reality I didn't say much. Today most people don't listen, they just talk. For a client it's often a breath of fresh air to find someone who listens. Becoming familiar with your clients' interests beforehand can even help you design a custom mural with personal touches, for example.

So, here's how I typically handle a meeting with a new client. When they answer the door I always introduce myself and shake hands, then wait to be invited in. Just basic courtesy, even though they know I'm coming and already know my name. At this point the client is either going to suggest we sit down to talk, or want to show me the room (or rooms) to be painted. It doesn't really matter which happens first. The key at this point is to do a lot of listening. When you look at the rooms, you can start to get an idea of the work involved, the colors that will be best, etc. Keep these things mostly to yourself for now. At some point of course you will sit down with the client and bring out your portfolio. While they look at your work, you are going to be quiet. Let them enjoy your work, don't feel the need to explain every photo. If they have a question, they'll ask. There may be a few photos that warrant a more detailed description or explanation, but on the whole you should **stay quiet**.

After the client has finished looking at your portfolio, he or she might be feeling overwhelmed by all of the possibilities. At this point I use my portfolio of sample boards to narrow down the choices. I usually have about 15 boards with me, in a combination of different finishes and colors. I hand them to the client and say, "Out of all these samples, take out the ones you don't like." Let's say of the 15 they remove 12. Now we're left with three different designs the client prefers. I then ask the client to look at the samples more carefully, maybe hold them up to a wall in the room, and choose the one(s) they like best. Once they've made a selection, I set that board, or boards, aside. I go through a gradual process of selecting the right finish for the client and the room. What I've done is controlled the situation while letting the client make all of the important decisions.

To select a color for the finish, I use the same basic process of elimination, but with a fan deck of paint colors instead of sample boards. You can get a fan deck at any paint store, sometimes free of charge, by asking the manager. So, you take out the fan deck, which has to be the most intimidating part of the process simply because of the sheer number of paint colors. I ask the client, "What colors were you leaning toward?" They might say, "Oh, green or yellow." Using the green and yellow sections of the deck, we then narrow down the choices just as we did with the finish samples. It usually doesn't take long at all for the client to choose one or two colors for me to create a sample for their job. Again, the client makes the decisions but you control the process.

The next step, of course, is to give the client a price for the work they choose to have done. For many artists this part of the process can be intimidating, but with experience and self confidence it will soon become second nature. I personally feel that it's important to quote a price right there on the spot so you can collect a deposit and book a date for the job. For the majority of commissions, this is entirely possible. If you're uncomfortable having the client looking over your shoulder while you figure a price for a job, suggest they look through your portfolio again while you look at the room and work out the numbers.

How you actually figure a price for a room and finish is up to your own personal comfort level. Many people have a price for each finish per square foot. They measure the square footage of the room, multiply it by the cost per sq. ft. of the finish, add on extras for obstacles such as windows and doorways, and come up with a total cost. I tend to treat it a little more simply. I look at a room as a ten by ten box, with 8 foot high walls, for example. I have a price for every finish for a room that size. Let's say I'd charge $500 for a glazed finish in a room that size. If the client's room happens to be 20 feet by 12 feet, I picture the room as two "boxes" and therefore double the cost to $1000. If the walls are 15 feet high then I might quadruple the price to $2000 plus some because of the height and difficulty. Breaking down the process of quoting a price into a simple process enables me to quickly tell a client how much I'll charge for the finish they want in a particular room of their home.

There are times when it is best to leave, figure out a price, and get back to the client. If, for example, someone wants multiple rooms painted in a variety of finishes with extras such as trim, or you need to work in the cost of special equipment like scaffolding, you might need to get back to them with a quote. When I have a job that is going to require several layers, a lot of detail, or multiple trips to a residence more than an hour from my studio, I need to take these things into consideration before giving a price. Go back to your office or studio, write up a complete work order with a room-by-room description of work to be done, and get back to the client with a price as soon as possible. I strongly recommend giving the client your quote in person if at all possible. This makes it easier to overcome any questions they may have or explore alternative finishes or designs.

Don't be afraid to quote a large price to a customer. When I give a client a quote, whether it's a hundred dollars or twenty

thousand dollars, I have the same look on my face. When you quote a price, don't defend it. You know how much your time and talent is worth, and the client knows they are paying for a custom luxury item. After you tell your client, "This job will be $12,000," close your mouth and don't say another word. Be casual and confident, and let them speak next. If you seem nervous about the cost, or scared they'll laugh and ask if you're joking, they'll sense an opportunity to bargain for a lower price. Think of it as playing a game, and the first person to speak loses. Many people won't bat an eyelash and will simply accept your costs, others will need a few seconds to let it all sink in. Just be patient.

Sometimes a client is truly surprised at the cost of a custom finish and isn't prepared to pay for the finish they initially choose. Be prepared to offer alternatives, such as a less-expensive finish in the same tones, or an accent wall instead of an entire room.

Once you have a finish, color, and price all worked out, the final step is to book a date for the work to begin. The way you handle this is crucial because your goal is to walk out of the meeting with a check or cash in your pocket and a firm date in your calendar. This is the key phrase: *"Right now we're booked out about three months. We try to treat our customers fairly, so work is scheduled on a first-come, first-served basis. In order to put your date in the book, we need a deposit of one-third the total cost. This also allows you to see as many custom samples as you want."* Now, they are either going to write you a check then and there, or they're going to waiver a little bit. You don't need to be pushy or try a hard sell, but casually tell them, *"The next date I have available could easily get pushed back. I have other meetings this week, so if you call me later to book a date, your job goes into the next available space on my*

calendar. I just want to make sure you're aware of that so you aren't disappointed when you call and I can't get in here quite so soon."
Most of the time that's all you need to say in order to close a deal. The client will pay you the deposit, you give them a date, and it's as simple as that.

I didn't start with this technique from day one of my business—it was something I developed over time. Asking for a deposit up front not only confirms that the client is serious about setting a date for the work to be done, it also protects my initial investment of time and effort. It took me about a year or so to develop my booking policies as they stand today, so if your own approach needs to be fine-tuned, stick with it and keep working at it. Growing into a better businessman or –woman doesn't happen overnight. Like I tell my daughter all the time, "We learn from our mistakes."

Another thing I make sure to point out to my clients is that the custom sample board I create for them is theirs to keep. Most people plan on purchasing coordinating room accents, new furniture, drapes, or rugs after the room is painted. Having a sample to bring to a store or show a decorator lets the client make purchases with confidence. Providing the sample to the client is an extra service we perform that doesn't really cost anything, is a convenience for the client, and makes us look good.

Mural Pricing

The "rules" for pricing murals vary so widely from job to job, and even state to state, that it's difficult to find a one-size-fits-all solution. There are some guidelines to take into consideration that should make the process simpler. First, I would suggest talking to other mural artists in your area and ask how they price their work. Answers will vary based on experience and level of expertise, but you should be able to get a good baseline reference.

Second, take into consideration your own level of experience and expertise. If you are just starting out and are still building your portfolio, your initial quotes for mural work may need to be more modest. As you develop your skills, take classes, and gain experience, your costs should change to reflect the higher quality of product you offer.

Lastly, when pricing a specific mural for a client, take into account every aspect of the job. Time spent on preliminary sketches, additional meetings to approve or fine-tune the sketches, the size of the mural, the complexity and level of detail, etc. Don't forget to ask yourself also how much your time is worth. How much do you need to make each day, or each week? I strongly suggest charging for your work by the job, not by the hour or by the day. If you finish the mural faster than you'd anticipated, you are still paid for your effort and skill. If the job takes longer than you'd expected, the client will not be surprised at a final price which exceeds your original estimate.

It is only natural that sometimes a client will want to make changes to a work in progress. Add a detail here, change a detail there, and before you know it you are spending more time and effort on a mural than you'd estimated. Make it clear, in as professional a manner as possible, that anything other than small changes may affect the price of your work. Clients should always sign off in writing on any changes to be made to the mural and the price.

Chapter 4

Staying Organized

Once you find yourself with three to six months' worth of work booked, things get very busy. Now you have a line of customers calling with questions or asking for consultations, samples to complete or redo, research for murals, and a myriad of other tasks constantly popping up throughout the day. Just when you think you have your schedule figured out for the next couple of weeks, a client calls to postpone because the contractor is behind schedule, or another client calls asking if you can get to them sooner because their baby arrived before schedule and the nursery isn't complete without that adorable mural you designed for them. Learning how to turn a juggling act into an effective and efficient schedule isn't a skill you have to be born with. Anyone can learn techniques to help them stay on top of things. I wasn't always organized or efficient, but I knew I needed to become those things in order for my business to reach its potential.

One drawback to having a busy schedule is that one job out of place can affect everything else. It's like the domino effect—if one job runs over, you have to call the next client and push back their date, then the next one, and so on, until you get some breathing room. I suggest working a day into your schedule as a cushion. Maybe not between every single job, but enough to prevent all of your clients from being inconvenienced if things aren't going smoothly. The upside is that you have the freedom to work longer days and even weekends to get your timing back on track. It will certainly help if you are already organized.

I start with a file for each client. In that file, I keep all relevant contact information such as names, phone numbers, address, driving directions, and email address. I also keep a job sheet in the file with information about the room, such as measurements, the colors used, pricing, and reference pictures. All I need is a quick glance through the file to have all of the information I need about that client.

These "open files" for current and upcoming clients don't sit in a file cabinet in my office. I keep them in a case in my truck so I have access to them even while I'm working. The clients expecting you in the next few weeks are most likely to call you during the day with questions or changes, and this way you don't have to call them back at the end of a long day, or try to remember the changes they asked for. Once the job has been completed, I file the information away in my office. I always have it to refer to in the future when the client calls back for more work or if they need a touch-up.

Another simple way to stay organized is to keep lists. I have three separate lists that I use to organize my work schedule. The first is a daily list of things I need to do and calls I need to make on that particular day.

Second, I have a weekly list. This one includes appointments and jobs or other deadlines.

Finally, I have a broader long-term list including all of my goals. This last list should always be in order of priority, and sometimes these priorities will change as new things come up. Instead of carrying around multiple slips of paper, a weekly or monthly planner with lots of extra room for notes (I'd suggest a three-ring style so you can add your own pages of notes or lists wherever needed) will keep you from losing information and also look professional.

If you can become super organized, you can appear to do the work of three people simply because you'll be able to efficiently multi-task. No matter how busy you get or how many distractions pop up, you'll be able to refer right back to your to-do list and stay on track. You'll be able to afford the luxury of sometimes being forgetful or flustered because your schedule, files, and lists will always be on hand to remind you where you're going and what you need to do next.

Keeping a disciplined daily schedule is also critical. If you like to sleep in and be home in time to eat dinner and watch the six o'clock news, you might find yourself without enough time in the day to work on one job and prepare for upcoming jobs. If you get an early start to your morning, put in a solid day's work painting for a client, and then spend even a little bit of time working on sample boards or preparing for the next day, you'll always be ahead of the game.

I try to schedule meetings with clients for early morning or late afternoon so I can get as much uninterrupted work done during the day as possible. Or, I'll fit in a meeting or two on the weekends. I can get them out of the way early and spend the rest of the day with my family. If you find a working rhythm that keeps you efficient and makes the most use of your time, you'll be able to accomplish more in a week than you imagine.

Chapter 5

Subcontracting and Hiring

W hy bother with hiring someone or sub-contracting? Look at it this way. While I was making money painting a mural at point A, I was also making money by having someone else do a faux finish at point B. I don't really like to have more than one person at the same job unless it's a large job.

My theory is that you can paint an entire room in a certain amount of time, but if you have two people painting a room it's not necessarily going to take half the time. Those two people are going to chat while they work or linger over lunch with some interesting conversation. If you spread those people out, you maximize efficiency.

It also doesn't make sense to have two people working on a small powder room or a relatively simple finish in one room. I realized that by having one person at one job while I work somewhere else, I could make the best use

of everyone's time. It also helps tremendously for last-minute jobs, where the client has a strict deadline and the work must be completed quickly. In this case, I bring someone in so we can finish the job on time. Having a trained painter you can trust to get a job done right gives you an invaluable amount of flexibility AND the potential to make more money for your business.

You will have to decide for yourself if you would be better served hiring someone to work for you, or subcontracting the work out. Once you find yourself with six months or more of work already booked, you can comfortably think of subbing out jobs. You'll need to find someone with special qualities, someone who is prepared to be with you long-term. There's nothing more frustrating that putting the time, effort, and money into training someone only to have them move on three months later.

From a physical standpoint, you'll obviously need someone who can handle strenuous work. Climbing up and down ladders, painting ceilings, lifting scaffolding, and lugging around equipment can all take a physical toll.

From a social standpoint, you want someone who represents your business well, has a professional manner and appearance (as professional an appearance as possible for someone who's usually covered in paint), and can verbally express themselves well. Anyone who works with you and for you should strive to maintain your business philosophy and policies. Whoever you hire is going to be face-to-face with your clients, representing your business for you. Keep that in mind when you begin to search for that person.

On top of the personal attributes I've already mentioned, it's essential to find someone with an excellent work ethic. I decided early on in my own search for that the ideal person to hire would have no initiative to start their own business, but would have great work ethic. These traits are very important. I have had a lot of luck hiring people with no training. I can teach them my own methods, primarily with respect to faux finishing.

Very simply, when I hire someone I need to know that they are happy. If they're happy, I'm happy. Many people take a management position and misuse it. It's not a dictatorship, it is a symbiotic relationship. Everybody, including yourself, deserves to be treated equally. If you can make your employees feel that they have value, you're off to a good start.

You'll have to decide for yourself between hiring someone as an employee or subcontracting out the work. I'd strongly suggest subcontracting to start with. Here's how it works. The person you sub work out to must have all the same paperwork and licenses for running a business. Their own business name, their own separate licenses. If you have an overflow of faux finish work that you subcontract out to this person's company, you pay their company.

Keep in mind that when you subcontract work, the person you're paying still has to file taxes. At tax time, you (or your accountant) will need to fill out a 1099 tax form. The form is available online.

Hiring someone as an employee is also an option. However, instead of your employee having his or her own business entity and licensing, you will need to have workman's compensation insurance, which works out to be 6% of your employee's earnings. You, as the employer, are responsible for this insurance. The forms and all necessary information are available on your state's website.

Next, of course, you need to work out how your employee or subcontractor will be paid. I start out paying a new hire 25% of the total cost of the job (after supplies). After three months, if all is going well, the pay rate goes up to 50%. I've always found it works best to pay on a percentage basis. For example, if I bid a job for a finish at $2000, first I take the cost of supplies off the top.

Let's say the supplies cost $200. The remaining $1800 is split evenly between me and the subcontractor. I don't have to worry about getting taken advantage of or losing money by paying someone hourly. The other benefit to this method of payment is it puts the responsibility for making money on the person I give the work to.

If the job takes a week, the pay is the same as if the job takes two days. It's completely up to the person I've hired to decide how much they want to work and how much money they want to make.

I've subcontracted much of my faux finishing work out to one person over the last several years, and this plan has worked beautifully. I sell the job to the client and make the samples. Once all the job details are worked out and the client has made an initial deposit, I hand the file over to my employee and he or she takes complete responsibility of the job from that point on. Any problems that come up on the job are his or her responsibility.

If the customer is not happy or if a spot was missed on a wall, my sub is responsible for fixing the issue before the job is considered complete and payment is made. This creates someone who will work quickly, because by doing so they make more money, and efficiently, because they are not compensated for time spent fixing mistakes.

Using this business plan with my subcontractors and employees has had some great benefits. One, it creates a deep sense of partnership and loyalty. I'm so grateful to the people I've worked with and strive to make sure they know how important they are. I also make sure they have a share in the success of the business through holiday bonuses and things like that. It's also very rewarding to see how someone who is trusted with the responsibility of handling every aspect of a job takes it seriously and works hard to maintain the standards I've set. Remember having someone else do the work for you creates a form of passive income.

Tip: subcontractors must be paid by three sources per year to be legitimate. If you have more than one company, you may pay them from each company to count toward that three. Also, consider sharing subcontractors with other faux companies.

Chapter 6

Going Above
and Beyond

One thing I've learned over the years is, you don't have to go to a lot of trouble to set yourself apart from others in the minds of your clients. First of all, they probably aren't artists if they're hiring you and the simple fact that you have the ability to paint something beautiful in their home will make you stand out in their minds. Second, each day you will have several opportunities to do small things that will guarantee clients think highly of you and talk about you to their friends. They'll not only pass on how great your work is, they'll gush about how great you are as a person.

Several years ago I started offering free touch-ups on any of my work, for as long as the client has the work in their home. Hearing about free touch-ups always peaks a client's interest and is a great selling point, even though I probably only do a couple of them each year. When I finish a faux job I leave the base coat and top coat at the client's house so it's available again if I need it. As a back-up, I keep all color information in a client's file as well. If they don't have the paint anymore when they call, I can stop and grab some more or mix a small amount of a color to match. Of course, the free touch-ups are for small nicks or dings that happen from day to day living. If someone throws a TV through the wall and wants it repaired, we're going to charge them.

If you offer this service to your clients, be sure they understand that the repairs are on your terms. On the rare occasions that I do get a call for a touch-up, I don't stop what I'm doing and rush over. I let the client know that I do touch-ups at my earliest availability. They may have to wait a couple of months before I can fit them in.

If a client calls for a touch-up and insists you come over that same day because they're having a party, you'll have to use your best judgment. If you can make it, go do it. You'll certainly make a lasting impression as someone who can be counted on in a pinch. If there is no possible way you can repair their walls that same day, keep a professional attitude and politely tell them you aren't available. Like I said, I don't get many calls to actually do touch-ups, but it is a nice service to offer and clients appreciate it.

Sometimes the ways you can go above and beyond are simple and spur of the moment. If you're working on a tall ladder and the client's chandelier or ceiling lights need new bulbs, offer to replace them while you're up there. It only takes a minute and your thoughtfulness will be long remembered.

Take the time to send a card to a client who's recently had a baby, or bring a baby gift if you're working in the home. Most of my clients have kids, and they love to watch me paint. I let them, and if I can do nice things for them as well, I try to do it. If I notice a child collects a certain kind of trading card, I might pick them up on my way to the client's house as a little surprise. One of my employees once even ended up babysitting for a client, which was a little strange but in an emergency situation meant a lot to the client. This is NOT something I'd recommend for liability reasons, however!

No one expects these things, but if you do them, your clients will tell their friends, I guarantee it. Now you're not just a great artist, you're a wonderful and thoughtful person. You can't underestimate how far small acts of kindness will take you.

After you finish a job, remind your customers every once in a while that you're still around. Keep a database of all customer information, and send holiday cards each year. Include a business card if you like, and possibly even a "coupon" as a gift to loyal clients. You'd be surprised how many past clients will call you for more work simply because your card reminded them of other things they want to do around the house. If you choose to send holiday cards, take advantage of the fact that the holiday season lasts until New Year's. If you want to be sure your card doesn't get lost in a rush of other holiday cards, mail them right after Christmas or just before New Year's.

Probably the most important aspect of going above and beyond is offering your clients superior customer service. For a decorative painter, this means being available to your clients, keeping your word, and providing a high-quality product.

If a client hires you to do a mural and you show up around noon, work until three, and take months to finish the project, chances are you won't be hired again or gain any referrals. If your clients can't reach you to approve samples, change a meeting date, or set up an appointment, they're going to simply hire someone else. Practicing excellent customer service means fixing any mistakes or problems immediately and without any hassle to your client. If you spill paint on the carpet (and haven't we all at some point?) take care of it yourself.

Your goal is to make the entire process a pleasure for your clients. Make their satisfaction your top priority and you can't go wrong.

Chapter 7

How to Work with an Interior Designer

By Sharon McCormick, Allied Member, ASID

Developing a network of interior designers who regularly refer jobs to you is an invaluable source of long-term revenue. Successful designers have a constant flow of high-end projects. The clients you get from interior designers should be the easiest sales to make. The client has already been pre-qualified, and you come with a glowing recommendation from an "expert." In addition, the design community is small and tight-knit, and we all discuss and trade resources, i.e., you!

I am often approached by artists who would like me to consider working with them, and some approaches are more successful than other. The best way is to make it a point to know something about the designer before you make a cold call. The more you know about the design business, and a designer's particular business, the higher your chances for getting an appointment. It is better to build a stable of designers you want to regularly do business with than to use a shotgun approach and try to get on board with every designer. You will find that there are a few designers you will love to work with, because their design sensibilities, level of clientele, business ethics, and temperament gel with yours. Just as in other areas of your live, you will find some relationships that won't click. Spare yourself heartache, and just move on.

The ASID (American Society of Interior Designers) has a chapter in each state with a corresponding website. The main website is **www.asid.org**. From here, you can do a search for designers in the zip codes where you would like to concentrate your business. Designers with an ASID designation are the professionals in the industry. In order to become a member, one has to have a college design education, meet experience requirements, and provide references. In some states, an exam is also required in order to obtain an interior design license.

Why is this important to the faux finisher? If you want to run a professional business, and you wouldn't be reading this good if you *didn't*, then it is in your best interest to associate with the cream of the crop. The expansion of HGTV and decorating magazines has led to a proliferation of people who abruptly hang out a shingle proclaiming that they are decorators without having any technical education or experience.

While it is possible to succeed with this approach, there will be much more training at the "school of hard knocks" than you will find with a seasoned professional, so carefully consider whether you want to be a part of that training. Depending on the size of your business, you will only be able to satisfy a limited number of designers, so why not align yourself with the best?

From the ASID website, you will find links to designers' individual websites. Take the time to review their portfolios before you make a cold call. Some designers tend not to use faux finishes or murals, so begin my concentrating your efforts on those who do. Is their work something you would like to be part of? Why? Be ready to engage in a knowledgeable conversation when you're ready to make that call. Be prepared to describe how you will be able to enhance *their* business.

A big turn-off for me is a cold caller who "is looking for work." I want to meet a faux finisher who is able to provide my clients and my business with something special, not someone who is looking for an easy way to make money.

Be sure to have your marketing materials ready before you make that all-important first phone call. In the design business, time is money. If you waste a designer's time, it is unlikely that you will get a second shot. Yours is a visual business, so be prepared to offer visual backup to your call.

A website is my first choice in reviewing an artist's work. Your goal is to ask the designer if he or she would like to view your website, and if this is a good time for her to bookmark it. If you can accomplish this during your cold call, you are much more likely to get results.

The better the pictures on your website, the higher your chances of getting an appointment with a designer. It is really important to take quality photos of your work as you go along. Many artists fail to do this, and it results in long-term lost income. The first step is to start with a clause in your contract stating that the client gives you permission to photograph your work (most people will be flattered). It is highly likely that you will have to return to a client's home at a later date to take pictures of your work to its best advantage. Make the time to do this—you'd be surprised how many other artists won't, and this will put you in a better competitive position.

A picture of a wall with a faux finish is boring, no matter how beautiful the finish is. Once furniture and artwork are moved back in, the photos become much more compelling. A tight shot will show the depth of your finish, while other objects in the picture are necessary to show scale. Keep in mind that there will be some jobs that may not photograph well, so use only the best in your portfolio. Keep your website updated, and change photos often.

Follow up the call by mailing your marketing materials. Include your business card, a brochure, color postcard or a chain set of finishes. Send these to the designer with a personalized letter. Designers get about 15 to 20 mailings every day! Make yours stand out. Creativity is your business, so use this as an opportunity to display it.

If there is a particular designer you *really* want to impress, offer to do some work for them *gratis*. Obviously, you can't do this for everyone, but designers who have been in business for a while will already have faux finishers that they are loyal to. You may need a drastic measure to get their attention, and this can be just the thing.

The absolute best (for you) would be to do a showhouse with them, giving you exposure to other designers as well as the general public. Next best would be to faux finish their offices or a room in the designer's home. If you go this route, kill yourself to get it right. Move the furniture, repair the walls, no delays, no complaining, no questioning—just do it and make it painless and you will likely have a fan for life.

Okay, so you have a designer on your team. Now what? Talent is only one part of the equation. There are a lot of broke faux finishers with talent! People skills are easily just as important in making a designer happy with your work. Remember, you approached us. Return our calls promptly. This is a simple thing, but it is surprising how often this is a stumbling block to a good relationship.

When I propose a faux finish to a client, the very first thing they ask is, "Do you know someone who can do it?" I say, "I know a really talented artist. I will call you tomorrow with a date when we can all meet." The client is very excited at this point, and we don't want to let that excitement dissipate.

It doesn't matter to me whether the artist can't meet for two weeks; the important thing is to make the appointment and get it on the client's schedule. You'd be surprised how many times a contractor won't call back until *they* are ready to meet, even after I've left multiple messages. By then, I've got a bad taste in my mouth and I've moved on to the second string. Who, by the way, has now become first string. I can't stress this enough—call the designer back as soon as humanly possible. They too are managing multiple projects and deadlines, and having to chase you shouldn't be one of them.

After having discussed the project with you, a meeting will be set up at the client's home. Again, simply courtesies apply. Be on time! Please! It is awkward for a designer to be apologizing for the tardiness of someone she has recommended. It is okay to look like an artist, but be professional. Have any materials you may need, and bring your portfolio. Unless the designer is specifically asking you for suggestions, never offer them in front of a client. You are being brought in to bid on the project that the designer has already specified. If you do have suggestions, offer them to the designer *after* your meeting with a client. There are numerous reasons for this.

First, the faux finish or mural is but one piece of the design puzzle. There are a myriad of other puzzle pieces, including furniture, fabrics, trims, and accessories, which have already been selected and "sold" to the client by the designer. While you may have a dynamite suggestion that the designer may not have considered, it is also possible that this suggestion may derail all of the progress she has made so far. This is a very fast way to make sure the designer never calls you again!

Second, the designer as already built a trust relationship with the client, often by spending numerous hours educating and priming the client to get to the point where they are ready to use you. Anything you do to chisel away at the client's reliance on the designer also chisels away at *your* relationship with the designer. While I am always eager and willing to listen to my faux finishers' ideas, I want to be able to give consideration to them in the comfort of my own office, rather than being put on the spot in front of a client. Changing things in the field is often where projects go awry, because of the domino effect of everything else that must change accordingly.

Next comes the estimate. Prepare it promptly, in writing, and submit it through the designer. Some designers will charge a mark-up on your work, so be aware that this may be an industry standard in your area. I do not charge a mark-up, and my contract specifies that all financial payments will be between my clients and the contractors. It is important that everyone is clear on who will pay you and when. However, I still prefer that the estimates go to my clients through me. I want to read the contract to be sure the artist and I are "on the same page" as far as the scope of the work to be performed, and to be able to change it if necessary before bothering the client.

Occasionally, I am still shocked by an artist's price, and I know if I am, the client surely will be! Usually this only occurs when I don't fully understand the job through the artist's eyes. Discussing it in advance, instead of getting a panicked all from the client out of the blue, helps me to sell or revise the job, to make it the best of all worlds for the artist, client, and the design integrity of the project.

Okay, everyone is excited—you, the designer, and the client. We, of course, want to know when! Please be very honest in your assessment of when you will be able to begin the project and how long you think it will take. Projects with designers are multi-faceted and detailed. There will be carpenters, painters, upholsterers, seamstresses, and installers, all carefully choreographed by the designer.

A sure way to upset a designer is to say you can start in four weeks, when you really won't start for eight weeks. Communication is key. We all know a previous project may take an extra day or two, but if you find this happening, call the designer immediately. Unbeknownst to you, other contractors may be unnecessarily working overtime to accommodate your schedule. The designer won't want to have to explain this to you, and it won't be necessary if you are realistic about your schedule and communicate any changes promptly.

When you arrive at the client's to start the job, be on time. If there is inclement weather, wear disposable booties to protect the client's floor. If you have a crew, use your best people on jobs for a designer. By best, I mean the most talented, the most professional, the most respectful. A client who uses a designer is likely used to a higher level of service than the general public expects, which means that the faux finisher needs to act accordingly. I've found that, while artists may be trained on the latest techniques, they do not receive training on interpersonal skills. This is a shame, because it is these skills that may make or break your business.

Ask the client if you may use their bathroom (I've had some clients ask the painters to go to a McDonald's!). Ask which sink to use for clean-up. If their children or pets are disturbing you, walk on eggshells when you gently explain that it is a safety issue (and that's about the only way you can approach it without offending anyone). Keep your voices down and mind your language. Be aware that some clients have webcams and are watching you at work! Don't say or do anything that you wouldn't if the client were right next to you. If you think of something that you feel will improve the job while you are in the field, call the designer to talk about it.

While we're on the subject of making changes, let's discuss what happens when the client sees you put the first stroke of yellow on the wall and freaks out. They insist on changing the color to beige, and so you do. Big mistake! While the client may be paying you, you are really working for the designer. Clients will occasionally have a panic attack, but don't let it throw *you* into a panic. Call the designer. Often it's just a simple matter of the designer reassuring the client. If you can't reach the designer and the client still wants to make changes, you will simply need to leave the job for the day until this can be resolved. Don't stress or yell. Just go back to your studio and prepare all of the sample boards you have been putting off.

Develop a long-term outlook on your relationship with the designer. Yes, this one job may be a loser, but by resolving issues calmly and to the satisfaction of the client, you will be assuring yourself a long stream of jobs from a grateful designer.

The first job Patrick and I did together was a disaster, and I take the blame! It was my very first client, too! I proposed a design, and Patrick, whom I had never even met, bid on the job. We went round and round with the client until we reached a "deal." The client was happy with the price, and off he went.

Well, Patrick did the job and I got an angry call from my client, who lived an hour away. I went up to see it, and it was, well, *sparse.*

What she had in mind was the original design, way before we got the price down (apparently I hadn't fully explained the new design to her). But, Patrick being Patrick, he traveled the hour and a half from his house to fix it, putting up the original design for a pittance of a price.

I spent all day watching him work, neither of us being paid. But he had a good sense of humor, lots of integrity, and a long-term outlook, and here we are today! Five years, many magazines, two showhouses and a book or two later, and he's still stuck with me!

There is one final way to ensure that a designer keeps referring work to you. Refer work back to the designer! Again, basic, but amazing how many contractors don't do this. You will be working in many, many houses. Your customer will bemoan the fact that they can't find the right draperies, or they're not sure what kind of rug will look best, or that the lighting in the room could be better.

That's when you pull out the designer's card and assure the client that you know just the right person to solve their problems! Ask your favorite designers about all of their capabilities, so that when an opportunity arises, you'll be prepared. Carry their cards as you do your own. Be the designer's biggest fan, and you will have a referral source for life.

Chapter 8

"Zero Budget" Marketing

If you're willing to be creative and think outside the box a bit, you'll find opportunities for basically free marketing all around you. Train yourself to see potential business everywhere, a potential client around every corner, and you'll be surprised how many doors open to you.

For example, just by talking about what you do, you can find new clients. I'm not suggesting you chase people around the grocery store, handing out business cards in the produce section or pitching someone in the frozen food aisle. You'll only scare people. On the other hand, if you find yourself making casual small-talk, even with a stranger, work your profession into the conversation. Every single time you'll be asked more detailed questions because what you do is far more interesting than what most people do. A few years ago I was at the airport with my family, waiting in a long line to check in at the airline's counter. The woman behind me in line started laughing at something one of my kids had done, and we began talking. In the course of the conversation I mentioned my business, which immediately grabbed her attention. She asked for my card and soon after called for a quote. It turned out she owned, with her husband, a successful chain of fast-food places and had recently built a new home. That one airport conversation led to thousands of dollars of work. That's only one example of how talking about my business earned more business. So, don't be shy, let people know what you do! Your confidence and enthusiasm about your work will naturally increase people's interest, which of course leads to more work.

Earlier in the book I briefly mentioned the potential to have newspapers and magazines promote your business free of charge. This is my favorite marketing technique because it looks great, attracts clients, and costs me nothing. All it takes is some enthusiasm and a little time on the phone. Let's say I'm painting a mural in a new restaurant. Before the job is complete, I call the local paper and say, "Hey, I'm painting this amazing mural at the new restaurant opening soon on Main Street. This place is going to be awesome, you really should have someone come down here and take a couple of pictures. I'll only be painting for another week or so, you can catch the work in progress or come out next week to see the finished product." I act excited and sort of cheesy, but it's contagious and it actually works. Most of the time the paper will send a photographer out to snap some shots, and a few days later, there I am in full color on the front page with a caption describing what I'm doing, where I'm doing it, and who I am. I've been in the newspaper many times for restaurant work, for restorations of local, well-known buildings, even a mural marking a town's anniversary celebration. If there's a local catch to the mural, the paper is much more likely to send out a photographer. But, you have to call them. Again, don't be shy! Keep in mind that the newspaper needs eye-catching photos and interesting stories, so when you hand them good material you're doing them a favor. Most of the time, the newspaper will use the photos either on the front page or on the front page of certain section. This way the photo will be in color. It will also be seen by more people because not everyone sits and reads the entire paper front to back. A big color photo with a nice caption is the best advertising you could ask for, and you aren't paying a dime for it.

As a side note, remember that most of the time the newspaper will have copies of the photos they used that they can give you either for free or for a small price. I'd suggest taking advantage of this if you like the photos simply because it's a good way to add some professional photographs to your portfolio.

The same basic principle applies to magazine articles. Look inside the magazine to find out who the editor is and just pick up the phone. Call or email, introduce yourself and state what you do. I'd suggest starting with regional magazines or publications. We recently had an article printed in Connecticut Home Interiors magazine that led to several calls from new clients, including one that landed a large job in a multi-million dollar home. It helps at this point if you can list other publications you've been featured in, even if they are small local papers. Don't be too modest, but keep a casual and friendly tone to the conversation. You'll be surprised at how many doors will open to you when you simply knock, and the money you'll be saving is literally insane.

Make it easy for other people to sell your work for you. When I approach a new decorator and want them to sell my work to their clients, I make it as easy as possible for them. I give them a professional portfolio specifically to show clients. This portfolio is a hard bound book created with an online digital photo processing company, which I talked about earlier. I also give them some of my cards and explain my policy of free touch-ups on faux finishes. The decorator not only sees that I'm professional, but also reliable, which makes it easy for him or her to sell my work to clients.

Another way to market yourself is to keep an eye out for new opportunities. If you're driving to a job and notice a new restaurant or business getting ready to open, don't be afraid to stop in with your portfolio. It might not lead to anything, or it could turn into a great lead. The first time I tried this method, I got the job. I'd noticed a new restaurant going up on a main street near another job site of mine. At the end of the day, I went inside with my portfolio and was lucky enough to find the owner in the building. I introduced myself, showed her my portfolio, and walked away with a deposit. Just because a business isn't officially "open" yet doesn't mean you can't go in and ask to speak to the owner, so don't be tempted to wait until the grand opening. By that time the space has been finished, patrons are milling around, and the owner is less likely to hire you because he'll have to run his business around you to some degree. Instead, walk right in with your portfolio and see what happens. You've got nothing to lose by introducing yourself and showing off your work.

Now and then I'll talk to another artist who has painted, or wants to paint, a wall in a place of business, free of charge, in order to attract more clients. The idea is to wow people with a great mural or faux finish and have business cards on-hand for anyone interested in contacting you for work. This can be an effective strategy, but only if you choose just the right business for such a display wall. You will also have to count on cooperation from the business in order to assure prospective clients are being given your contact information. Honestly, I hate to do free walls. That said, I have done them with great success. Here in Connecticut we have some huge granite and tile show rooms, the kind where all the interior designers send their clients. In one of these show rooms, we concentrated on a twenty-foot high wall that spanned about one hundred feet across. We broke the wall up into sections and did seven or eight different finishes on it. At one end of the wall, we painted a quick mural. I then had a ten-foot sign made (this is something you could probably do yourself if you truly want to keep your budget small) and hung it right in the center of the wall. It's visible from every spot in that show room. We actually got quite a few calls because of that wall, most of them in the two to four thousand dollar range. We also got one outstanding client who not only booked us for over $15,000.00 worth of work, but referred us to everyone in her neighborhood. Remember when I talked about "connectors?" This client has certainly connected us, to the point where several months down the line we are still doing work in her area based solely on word-of-mouth from this one client who saw the wall we painted in the show room.

The key to the success of this free wall was the clientele. People were there for home improvement, saw first-hand the various finishes alongside the granite and tile, and could instantly visualize possibilities for their homes. Unless you have the opportunity to showcase your work in this particular type of establishment, you may not see an overwhelming response. As another artist pointed out to me, people go to a restaurant to eat and relax, they go to a dentist or doctor with trepidation, but they go to a home improvement store for home improvement. You have to catch people when their minds are already on improving their living space. If you decide to do a public space for free, keep that in mind when selecting a location and you won't be disappointed. To find just the right business, get in touch with some interior designers in your area and ask where they send their clients for tile, countertops, etc. Most likely they can even introduce you and put in a good word for you if they've done work with you in the past. Also, don't be shy about walking into a business and introducing yourself. It's a win-win situation because you benefit from new clients, and the business gets a beautiful finish or mural free of charge.

Finally, you should never, under any circumstances, underestimate the importance of word of mouth advertising. The vast majority of my business comes from word of mouth—one client giving my name to a friend, relative, or co-worker who then gives my name to someone else, who gives it to someone else, etc. Every aspect of the way you work with your clients influences the way they will speak of you to others. If you are honest and responsible, go above and beyond, and always follow through with what you say you're going to do, you will find more and more business coming your way simply through referrals.

Once you've built up a solid customer base through a good mix of traditional and creative marketing methods, you should see a steady stream of work from referrals and even repeat customers coming in. Reaching this stage of business should be your top goal. I'm not saying you'll eventually get to a point where you don't need to market yourself at all, but you should be able to reach a level of business where a good portion of your new clients approach you at the recommendation of your previous clients.

Chapter 9

Thinking Outside the Box

P art of becoming a successful small-business owner, no matter the type of business, is thinking outside the box. This saying has been overused to the point of becoming a cliché, but it truly applies to the mindset you need to make quick decisions that benefit your business in the long run.

Sometimes decisions you make should not be about money. Before walking away from a customer who can't afford your work, take a minute to think of any long-term benefits to doing the job anyway. If the client wants an enormous and detailed mural in their basement but has a budget of a hundred dollars, you'd mostly likely say no or drastically reduce the scale and complexity of the mural.

On the other hand, if a client has an amazing space and you have a brilliant idea to go with that space, sometimes it's better to accept less money than you're worth for the opportunity of adding that job to your portfolio. Here's an example. Several years ago a restaurant owner called me for a quote on a ceiling mural. The restaurant had a very large domed ceiling in the main dining room which the owner wanted to accentuate with a mural. His budget, however, didn't leave a lot of room for the imagination. I had to make a choice—I could paint a simple design, such as a mariner's compass, on the dome. It would only take a few hours and would be worth what he could pay me.

On the other hand, the dome was so obviously deserving of something spectacular that I truly did not want to pass up the chance to paint such a space in the best way possible.

I also realized the potential of having a stunning piece of art in a public area, seen daily by scores of possible clients. In the end, I decided the long-term benefits of painting an eye-catching mural on that dome far outweighed the inconveniences of taking a temporary pay cut.

I painted a beautiful mural of balustrades, cherubs, and clouds in the dome. The local newspaper printed a photo of it on the front page along with an article about my business. Between the newspaper article and the restaurant patrons who asked the owner for my card, I more than made up for money I didn't make by doing that job.

Sometimes it isn't a client's budget that forces you to make a decision with long-term effects, but his or her attitude. A few years ago I had a client who wanted their foyer walls painted to look like stones. They had already met with a couple of artists who could not do the job, but I took it on.

The foyer was stunning as it was, with two story-high, rounded walls and a dramatic curved stairway. I always charge a flat fee for a job, not by-the-hour. I gave the clients my price and estimated the entire job to take two weeks.

I actually finished the job a bit faster than I had expected, and when the client saw the foyer (which looked amazing), we had a conversation that went like this:

Client: "I'm not comfortable paying you this amount of money for the job."

Me: "Excuse me?"

Client: "Well, you said it would take two weeks, and you finished four days early."

Me: "I estimated it would take two weeks. Things went along faster than I expected. As I explained, I charge a flat rate for my work regardless of how long the job actually takes."

Client: "Well, if you were a good businessman you'd charge me less. I'd expect to pay more if you spent three weeks here instead of two weeks. Since you finished early, I expect to pay less."

Me: "I am a good businessman. I live up to my word. I gave you a price, and I stick to that price, even if it had taken me three weeks. I would not have charged you more money because we had already agreed on a price."

Client: "Well, like I said, I'm not comfortable with paying you the full amount."

At this point I know that I can keep arguing with him and get the full commission if I want to. I have a contract that he signed agreeing to pay a certain amount for the work I'd done. I also know that if I play rough and insist on getting my money from him, he will not let me back into the house with a photographer. I'd be lucky to get back in with a disposable camera, for that matter. While we're having this conversation I'm looking around at this gorgeous foyer, already seeing the breathtaking photos of it in my portfolio. I had to make a decision on what was best for my business in the long run.

I swallowed a bit of my pride, cut back the price, and left the job with some of the most impressive photos in my portfolio. Every time I show my work to a new client or designer, they ooh and ahh over that foyer. I can't even tell you how much work that photo has gotten me. If I'd argued with my client, insisted on getting every penny owed to me, and left on bad terms, he would have refused to let me back in for photos. Who can say how many jobs that foyer has landed me? I lost a bit of money in the short term, but more than made up for it in the long run.

Of course, several months later the same client called me for more work, and I turned him down. Under no circumstances was I going to work for him again. So while you may have to make some tough choices when dealing with a client, you by no means have to put yourself back into that position again. I refused to work with that client again, but if you find yourself in the same position and decide to work with someone like this a second time, don't forget to add in the PITA (Pain In The Ass) charge!

Don't get me wrong and think I'm suggesting that you have to either work for less money than you deserve or put up with clients who want to push you around or take advantage of you. Most of the time, I'd rather walk away from a problem job than put up with it, but it's important to always take time to consider the long-term benefits to sticking with a less-than-ideal situation.

However, when you do encounter a client who is making you miserable or can't be pleased, there are certain ways to handle yourself. If a client doesn't pay me when I'm supposed to get paid, I don't work. If a check bounces, the job isn't finished until I have cash in hand. I'm not unreasonable, but my time is very valuable and I'm not going to spend it working on a job that I suspect I might not get paid for.

When I have a client who is too overbearing, nitpicks, and argues, I bite my tongue as best I can, finish the job, and simply don't work for them again if I don't want to. I once had a client who drove me crazy in several ways. She'd hired me to paint quite a few rooms in her home for literally tens of thousands of dollars. When the job was finally finished, I couldn't wait to get out of her home. So of course, she wanted a quote for a finish in her foyer. I didn't want to work with her again, but didn't want to come right out and tell her that. Instead, I had the brilliant idea to give her a quote so obviously inflated that she'd never agree to it. I told her I could do her foyer, gave her a price that, to me, seemed unacceptable, and expected her to change her mind. I swear to God, she didn't even blink but just asked when I'd be able to fit the job in. My plan backfired, but at least that time I was well-compensated for putting up with a problem client. Just use your judgment when you run into trouble and handle the situation the way you feel is best for your reputation. Don't do things you wouldn't want other clients to know about.

Let me give you another example. Let's say you finish a job and the client owes you a final payment of $1,050. The customer mistakenly gives you a check for $1000. Should you tell the customer he owes you another $50? A lot of people are going to say yes, you deserve it. I would say no. I think it leaves a negative impression to come back to a client for a measly fifty bucks. I would not call a client on the phone or go back to the door and say, "You know what, you're fifty shy." I would rather keeps things on a positive note and just let it go. If the client erred by more, I'd certainly say something, but if it's a small amount I don't even worry about it.

If I'm doing a large job and they're spending a lot of money, tens of thousands of dollars, and they decide they want me to paint a door for them, I'm probably going to do it free of charge. I'm not going to nickel and dime somebody just because I'm making a lot of money. I think of it like that. Of course, there's a limit, and before you find yourself assembling the family's Christmas tree (which actually happened to another artist I know), be ready to say no politely and firmly. Adding a touch here and there onto a lucrative job is one thing, doubling your work without being compensated is something entirely different.

Online Resources

Use the Internet. There are online resources available to you that will truly help you grow as an artist. You can chat with other decorative artists or post on message boards. In 2006 I developed The Faux Forum at www.fauxforum.com. Many of the most talented and experienced mural and faux artists from around the world contribute regularly to this forum and are so generous in their help to others. It's a great place to learn about different techniques and products, ask others to critique your work, or just have a few laughs.

The Faux Forum also allows members to create an Art Space page featuring their work. It's very user-friendly, and there's no cost for membership. In addition to the Forum, I've developed www.learntofaux.com with online galleries, tutorials, and listings of decorative painting schools all over the country. The Internet also allows you to find images to inspire murals, research different areas of decorative painting, and even design an email campaign targeted to your clients. Take advantage of the technology that's available, as most of it is invaluable and easy to access.

Using the Internet and email to keep in touch with clients also opens the door to another method of marketing that can work very well. Be sure to keep your clients' email addresses on file, and once you've generated a decent list you can send out regular e-newsletters. These can be sent out on a schedule of your choosing, depending on how often you'd like to update clients on your business. You certainly don't want to annoy people, so I'd suggest only using this option if you have something truly worth passing on to your past clients.

I use a company called Constant Contact (www.constantcontact.com). It's very simple to use. You input email addresses and fill out an online form which creates a professional-looking newsletter, complete with photos. This newsletter is emailed to everyone on your list. You can then go online to see how many people are clicking on links in your newsletter, how many are deleting it without reading, etc.

Anyone who doesn't want to receive the newsletter can "unsubscribe" automatically. I'd suggest using the newsletter to promote new techniques or showcase a special job you've done, such as a mural in a high-profile restaurant. If you decide to expand your business to include a line of stencils, put it in a newsletter. You'd be surprised how many people will call you for more work simply because your newsletter kept you on their minds.

Chapter 10

Website Development

With Matthew Grimm

S hould you have a website? Yes. I feel very strongly that a website is an essential tool for a decorative painter. You probably won't ever get a lot of direct work from it, but having an online portfolio and web presence is necessary. If you do a job for a client, that client can instantly show your portfolio to a friend or co-worker by giving them your web address. Or, if you get a call from someone and aren't available to meet with them for a week or two, you can give them your website. They have the opportunity to see your portfolio online, which keeps them interested and gives them ideas for when they do meet with you in person. Finally, having a website makes you look more professional and established. In fact, it is almost expected for you to have a web site and for that site to be listed on your business card.

So how do you get a web site, and what do you put on it? Believe it or not, it can be a fun and rewarding process. Even if you know nothing about web site development, you can build a professional and personalized web site featuring your work. The first step is to find a web designer. Before you hire a web designer, you'll want to have a good idea of what you'd like your website to convey. You don't necessarily need to know the specific design, but having some examples of websites you like (or those you don't) and a general idea of the colors and themes is a great start. Communicating your vision to a prospective designer helps ensure an accurate estimate of cost and generally moves the process along at a faster rate.

Before hiring a web designer, shop around. Odds are someone you know has used a web designer and might be able to recommend someone to you. Check out the designer's portfolio to see if his or her style matches what you have in mind for your site. Ask the designer for references and, if possible, contact them. You can ask how their overall experience was while working with the designer. Also, ask the designer how changes to the initial website will be handled. Most likely, if you want to change text or images down the road, you can do so using a WYSIWIG editor. It's a technical sounding thing, but your web designer should make sure that you, as owner of the site, are able to do this. If you do need to make bigger changes to your site, work out with the designer what the charges for additional work or updates would be. And of course, you'll want to take the initial cost into consideration as well. This is also a good time to work out a contract with your designer whereby he or she provides you with all work materials (images, text, code objects, flash source code, etc.) at various agreed-upon milestones during the project. This ensures that if your designer goes AWOL, you have something a new designer can use without having to redevelop all of the original work. Logos and flash objects can be very costly to redevelop, so keeping a copy of these for yourself can save you inestimable amounts of time and money down the road.

You'll also need to get a domain name. This is your web address. Mine, for example, is www.creativeevolution.net. Your domain name ideally would be the same as your business name. Keep in mind that the domain name should be as short as possible and end with top-level domains such as .com, .net, .org instead of .biz, .info, .us, etc. To see if a domain name is available, you can look it up on a website such as www.checkdomain.com. If the domain name you want is available, you should register it as soon as possible. To register a domain name, go to www.dns.com and click on "Domain Registration." You will be given a list of companies that offer domain name registration. This is certainly something you can do yourself, but it's sometimes a good idea to see if your web designer offers to register the domain name at a reasonable cost. Your designer might also handle hosting, which I'll explain about later. There's an added value to having one point of contact for all of these things.

Now, serious mistakes can be made at this initial step. Here is a real-world example of a domain name registration gone terribly wrong: Client is referred to or otherwise locates a web designer. The web designer offers to register the domain name on behalf of the client. One year later, the client loses touch with the original designer. Upon finding a new designer, the client discovers that the domain name he registered is about to expire. He then learns that the domain record lists the original designer as the owner of the domain name. This is big trouble, because only the registrant (owner) can renew or transfer the domain.

Moral of the story: Be aware that once you register your domain name you do have to renew it AND the domain **must** be registered in your name in order for you to do this. Yeah, your designer can do it for you, but just in case, make sure it is in your name. Assuring that you are the official registrant of your new domain name is easy enough to do, even if you do have your designer or host register and manage it. You can verify the record is accurate by visiting **www.whois.sc**.

When you (or your designer) register a domain name you'll want to make sure you have a login to control the domain record. This domain control panel enables you to update contact information (registrant, administrative, and technical) and name servers.

A great new option to consider is setting your domain to auto-renew each year. This eliminates the need to register for multiple years and just about eliminates the risk of your domain ever expiring on you. An expired domain can be very difficult to reclaim. Some registrars will give you a grace period (sometimes referred to as a redemption period), and then place your domain in a limbo status, where neither you nor anyone else can register it. This period can last for up to 90 days and varies from registrar to registrar.

I would also keep an eye out for the "loss leaders" in the domain name market. They usually offer domain name registration at a very low rate, in the hope that you will buy other, mostly unnecessary, services from them. Others may offer a "first year" price, but renewal rates might actually exceed the average market price for a domain.

Once you have a domain name registered, you need to find a web host. A web host stores your web pages, images, and databases on a server and presents them on the Internet. Web hosts also administer and manage the email for your website if you choose to use that feature. Selecting a host is also something your web designer can most likely help you with and even manage, but I think it's always good to be prepared with the information so you understand the difference between good quality and poor quality. Your web site is an important business investment, and like any other investment, deserves a certain amount of research.

When choosing a host, you want to know that your data is safe, secure, and located in a professionally managed environment. This usually means the server is located in a Data Center. I strongly recommend avoiding any host with servers located in a residential setting. A Data Center has several distinct advantages over a residential or other non-Data Center facility. You'll want to look for a host with 24/7/365 monitoring and support. They should also have back-up power, usually in the form of diesel generators. Sure, a residential setting can have a generator, but will they have a supply of fuel guaranteed in the event of a disaster? Your hosting service should also have multiple ISPs (most have at least two different ISPs), which are the backbones to the Internet. Finally, the Data Center should have raised floors and fire suppression. Floods and fires happen, so knowing your host is protected as best as possible is reassuring.

In addition to the physical location of your hosting service, there are other aspects to take into consideration. The best way to quickly find the answers to the following questions is to read the provider's SLA (Service Level Agreement). This is usually a 1-2 page document that outlines the expected service level and any refunds due to you in the event of extended downtime. If the host doesn't have an SLA, I'd suggest moving on. The questions to ask (and reasonable answers) are:

Q: **How often is the server backed up and what is the restore policy?**

A: Ideally, you'd like to have a full backup of your website daily. Websites with forums, blogs, or other database-driven content need daily backups. However, if your content does not change daily, then a weekly backup is usually fine.

Q: **What is the uptime history of the server your site will be hosted on?**

A: Web hosts should be able to tell you the most recent uptime statistics for the server your website will be hosted on. Uptime is a measurement of how long a server has been up (and by "up" we mean accessible to visitors), usually reported in %. A good uptime score is 97% or better.

Q: **What is the response time during an emergency?**

A: When the server becomes unavailable, is someone available onsite? You'll want to check the host's SLA to see if they guarantee hardware replacement times or data restores (in minutes/hours). You'll want to avoid a hosting situation where the server is not monitored, or replacement parts & personnel are not available on-site.

Q: **Are parts available on-site to repair a down server?**

A: In the event of a catastrophic hardware failure (ie. hard drive, power supply, motherboard, etc.), does the host have identical replacement parts available to bring that server back on line? Most data centers will have a ready supply of parts.

Q: **Congestion - How many other websites are currently on the server?**

A: I don't like to see hundreds of websites on a single server. A server only has so many resources to allocate.

Q: **What is the maximum number of sites that will be hosted from this server?**

A: I would recommend avoiding a server with more than 300 websites. To see how many websites are sharing the same IP, you can do a "whois" lookup at www.whois.sc. Check under the "Reverse IP" option to see how many other websites share the same IP (server).

Note: This is not a perfect tool, as there could be other websites hosted on the same server using a different IP.

Like I said, much of this can be handled or facilitated by your web designer if you decide to work with one. Knowing what to expect from domain name registration and web hosting, however, will help you make sure you are getting the quality you want and the level of service you're paying for.

Finally, you get to the fun stuff! The actual design and layout of your website can be really exciting to build. The final look of the site is completely up to you, but I'd suggest keeping a few design considerations in mind. After all the work you put into a website, you want it to be an accurate reflection of your artistic ability and level of professionalism. The website should be well-organized and easy to navigate. If you want other opinions on the site as it develops, you can have friends (or anyone who will give you an honest opinion), check out the work-in-progress and offer tips on making it user-friendly. Content on your site is great, but avoid presenting too much information. The main feature of your site should be your portfolio. A page with contact information, as well as a page with brief descriptions of the services you offer, can answer questions for potential clients without overwhelming them. Make sure your text is easily readable against the background color or image. I also suggest avoiding background music. Your visitor might be in a situation where they didn't expect to broadcast what they were looking at. If you do decide to use music, be sure there is a button to click in order to turn it off.

Your online portfolio can be arranged any way you choose, but I feel it makes the most sense to present your work by type. For example, a gallery of murals, a gallery of faux finishes, a gallery of children's rooms, etc. Visitors should have the option of clicking on an image to see a larger version. This is where taking notes on sites that appeal to you will come in handy. If you know what works well and you know what you like, you can work with your designer to build a site that will also appeal to your clients.

Your website should also include a link to your email address. Some clients will prefer to contact you this way. Check your email daily and respond quickly!

Finally, I'd like to talk about Search Engine Optimization, or SEOs. Your website should be built from the start with SEO in mind. Depending on the audience you most want to reach, your web designer can help with this technical and often confusing subject. If you plan to only offer your services locally, as the vast majority of decorative artists do, then it will most likely make sense for you to build your site with local searches in mind. For example, a Google search for "San Diego faux finish," if you live in San Diego, should lead clients to your site. However, if you expand your business at some point to include products, such as stencils, or decide to offer classes in decorative painting, you'll want to reach a wider range of people.

This doesn't mean that you shouldn't work with a great designer if he or she lacks the SEO skills to optimize your site, it just means that you might want to consider hiring an SEO professional BEFORE your designer starts coding your website. You can instruct your SEO pro to work with your designer to appropriately develop the site from the start.

Be very careful of anyone who claims to know exactly what does and does not work in the ranking game. SEOs change rapidly and you want to work with someone who is constantly learning and adapting to changes.

Ask your web designer to incorporate the following bot-friendly elements ("bots" search your site for relevance to search terms):

1. Custom TITLE tags on each page. These are the words that appear in the top blue bar of your browser.

2. ALT descriptions for all images. Alternative descriptions were implemented for visitors with accessibility issues or images turned off. Search engines read these tags as content and are useful with Google images, etc.

3. META tags. These are web page elements not viewed by the visitor, but used to describe information about a web page to different bots, spiders, and other agents. Each search engine has different policies with regard to how these tags are used and not used. For example, Google reportedly does not use the "keywords" tag, whereas Yahoo does.

4. H1 tags for headings. This is a design element that your web designer incorporates when adding content to your pages.

In general, I usually enjoy quick success with Yahoo and MSN search engines. Google, not so much. Google has a component to its ranking called Page Rank, and the lower your site's Page Rank is, the lower your site ranks in the search results.

I have some general information to share that I think is important for everyone to see. There tends to be a lot of questionable advice out there (especially among us small business types) that leads one to believe we can manipulate our ranking in the SERPs by employing certain tactics, often deceptive ones. Be careful of using "tricks" to increase your ranking with SEOs, because it's hard to say specifically what will get you into hot water with the search engines, but there are plenty of old tactics that have become fairly useless.

One technique people still ask me about is hiding text, stuffed with keywords. This used to be a very prevalent practice (and it actually worked for a while). However, it is now ignored by Google. I'm not sure if doing this will get you sandboxed or anything, but it won't help you either.

Another fairly useless endeavor (though I do it when clients insist) is to cram hundreds of keywords into the keyword META tag. Of the few search engines that still use META tags (for ranking purposes), most employ either a keyword relevancy check (they compare your content to your META keywords to see which ones appear in the body of the page most frequently and toss the others out) or they limit how many characters in the keyword tag they will read.

A low ranking is more often the result of not doing something versus doing something bad. Outside of covering the bases with META tags, here are a few heavy hitters that should be focused on when optimizing your website:

1. Content is king. A good mix of text, images, and links is always a good thing. You don't have to go crazy and write a book. It's more important that the text you do have is relevant to your TITLE and META information (and also the search terms you are trying to rank well for).

2. TITLE tags are very important (at least in Google). Unless your domain name is the search term you are trying for, don't bother putting it in the TITLE tag. Each page should have its own **relevant** TITLE tag.

3. ALT tags (and the lesser known title tag) for images should describe the image (and of course contain some targeted keywords). Don't go crazy here either. There is likely a limit as to how far the tag will be read by the search engine.

4. Upload a Robots.txt file to the root directory of your website. This tells the bots where, and where not, to go.

5. Get your site in the DMOZ.org. This is a human-edited directory, and being listed here carries weight with some search engines, namely Google.

As a word of caution, don't try to cheat the search engines. They may be a step behind here and there, but they always catch up. If your site gets "sandboxed" or "de-listed" because they caught you hiding text, links, or whatever, you'll be kicking yourself.

Finally, check with the best resource available for SEO optimization, which is Google itself. The more you learn about what works and doesn't work, the more prepared you'll be to work with an SEO pro or take on the job yourself. The following sites are wonderful resources:

1. Google Webmaster Guidelines. This is a very important page. Google tells you everything you need to know to help your ranking. www.google.com/support/webmasters/bin/answer.py?answer=35769

2. Google Webmaster Tools. www.google.com/webmasters/

3. Matt Cutts (from Google) has a blog. He often uses it to discuss Google updates, as well as dispel nasty SEO rumors. www.mattcutts.com/blog

4. Some other great websites with SEO tools and opinions: www.searchenginewatch.com and www.seochat.com

I know much of this information is very technical and can seem overwhelming to someone new to website design. My goal in providing this information is to prepare you to not only work with a designer and/or SEO professional, but to help you be aware of the services you should look for and the things people working on your site should or should not be doing. At the end of the day, I hope you find yourself with a beautiful and professional site that inspires your clients and shows off the best of your abilities.

Chapter 11

Conclusion

In closing, let's talk about one more thing that will enable you to stand out from, and above, the crowd. Three words: motivation, desire, and energy. What exactly do these words mean? More specifically, what do they mean to you? Everyone has a different answer, but knowing your own mind and heart is critical to your success in your own business.

Motivation: the ability to be able to make action under any circumstances. I'm not sure if Webster would define it just like that, but for me, it's ideal. To be able to push and move forward whether you are surrounded by good fortune or bad, whether your goal seems simple or almost unattainable. What motivates you? For me, it is my wife and children, my dream that I am more than I am. It's feeling like the possibilities of the future are under my control and that my destiny is determined by my actions. I enjoy the fight of the job, putting out fires and creating allies around me, building a team of like-minded peers. I am motivated by the unknown, and by a strong aversion to the word "No." Motivation has a different face for everyone, but you shouldn't have to look far to find yours.

Desire: What is the desire of your life? I have always had many. Overall, I see myself down the road as an older man who can look back and say that I feared nothing and tried to succeed in all my endeavors. I don't want to regret things that I wanted to do, but didn't. I was once asked if I'd rather have money, success, or notoriety. Well, I'd want to have them all! Why not? From this desire, I fuel a part of my motivation and my energy.

Energy: To some, this is 8 hours a day, and to others it's 4. Imagine two individuals, one with the gift of intelligence and one with the ability to keep moving forward in spite of obstacles, setbacks, or mistakes. Energy can sometimes create the same outcome as intelligence. The two together are an unstoppable force. To me, energy means being the last one on the phone at night and the first one working in the morning. It means spending all day climbing up and down scaffolding after being woken up every hour the night before by a stubborn toddler. Energy also means multi-tasking, doing the work of four people. Not necessarily physically, but by taking calls while I'm painting or driving, stopping at my studio on the way home each day to catch up on emails, sample boards, and phone calls. Energy means to do more than most and push harder.

Being able to combine your motivation, desire, and energy and draw on their inspiration to achieve your goals will not only help you get through the rough times, but will ensure that you continue to grow as an artist and a businessperson. The amount of success you have is, in a very large part, determined by how much of yourself you are willing to give to your business. The principles

I've put forward in this book have consistently worked for me over the past several years, and I know they'll work for anyone who has the drive to put it all together and work toward long-term goals. It's not always easy, but the bright side is getting to do what you love, making your clients speechless with wonder and delight at how you've transformed their home, seeing a kid's entire face light up at a fantastic mural, and knowing that you are working toward living your dream.

Most of all, enjoy the challenge, enjoy the opportunities to learn and create something that wasn't there before—your own unique business based on your own unique talent and style for decorative painting.

Sample Contract used –

Check with lawyer for applicability in your state.

[CREATIVE EVOLUTION LETTERHEAD]

Home Improvement Contractor License #_____

[DATE]
[NAME]
[COMPANY]
[ADDRESS]
[ADDRESS]

Dear [NAME]:

Thank you for your interest in the services of Creative Evolution, LLC ("Creative Evolution"). This letter reflects the terms upon which you have agreed to retain Creative Evolution.

Creative Evolution will provide the following: _____
_____
_____ (the "Work").

The Work will be performed at _____[location]_____ (the "Premises"). Creative Evolution shall start the Work on ____[date]____, and the Work shall be completed no later than _____[date]____ (the "Completion Date").

The Work performed, designed or created hereunder shall remain the sole property of Creative Evolution for all purposes, including, but not limited to, copyright, trademark, service mark, patent, trade secrets and other intellectual property laws, and the Work shall not constitute a work for hire pursuant to 17 USC 201. Creative Evolution hereby grants to you a paid-up, royalty-free, non-exclusive license, revocable at will, to display the Work at the Premises into perpetuity.

In consideration of the above, you agree to pay to Creative Evolution a total price of: _____. A deposit of one-third of the total price is due and payable from you to Creative Evolution immediately upon your execution of this Agreement. A second payment of one-third of the total price is due and payable from you to Creative Evolution on or before ____[date]____. A final payment of the balance of the total price is due and payable from you to Creative Evolution immediately upon delivery of the Work.

All work performed by Creative Evolution shall be performed in a workman-like manner. Any alterations or deviation from the work to be performed by Creative Evolution as described in this letter shall be mutually agreed upon and set forth in a writing, signed by you and Creative Evolution, and may result in additional charges to you.

You agree that, after the Completion Date, Creative Evolution may re-enter the Premises at a mutually agreed upon time to video, photograph or otherwise view and/or record the Work, and you shall not unreasonably withhold your agreement to the same. You agree not to permit third parties to video, photograph or otherwise reproduce the Work without the prior written consent of Creative Evolution.

You agree to pay all costs, including reasonable attorneys' fees, incurred by Creative Evolution to enforce the terms of this Agreement. This Agreement shall be governed by the laws of the state of Connecticut, without regard to conflict of law rules.

Creative Evolution is a registered Home Improvement Contractor with the State of Connecticut, and is fully insured. The relationship of Creative Evolution to you is that of an independent contractor. Nothing herein contained shall be deemed to authorize or empower you, your agents or employees, to act as agent for Creative Evolution or conduct business in the name, or for the account of, Creative Evolution or any of it's affiliates, or otherwise bind it or them in any manner.

No failure or omission, in whole or in part, to carry out or observe any of the terms, provisions or conditions of this Agreement shall give rise to any claim against Creative Evolution or be deemed to be a breach of this Agreement, if the same is caused by or arises out of force majeure. To the extent that it is not within the reasonable control of Creative Evolution, the term "force majeure" as used in this Agreement shall mean hostilities, acts of the public enemy, acts of terrorism, disease, public disorder; acts of Government; acts of God or the elements; failure of transportation, equipment or facilities; unavailability of supply, labor disturbances, and any other cause whether or not of a similar nature provided that it is beyond the reasonable control of the party thus prevented from performing its obligations hereunder, which would have the effect of preventing and/or impeding the performance of Creative Evolution in accordance with the terms of this Agreement.

[NAME]
[DATE]
Page 3 of 3

If you are in agreement with the above terms, please manually execute each of the two (2) copies of this letter, and return one fully executed copy to Creative Evolution together with your initial one-third deposit. Please keep one fully executed copy of this letter for your permanent records.

We look forward to working with you.

Very truly yours,
CREATIVE EVOLUTION, LLC

By: _____

Patrick C. Ganino, Member

Agreed and accepted this ____ day of _____ , 2003.

_____

[NAME]

YOU, THE BUYER, MAY CANCEL THIS TRANSACTION AT ANY TIME PRIOR TO MIDNIGHT OF THE THIRD BUSINESS DAY AFTER THE DATE OF THIS TRANSACTION. SEE THE ATTACHED NOTICE OF CANCELLATION FOR AN EXPLANATION OF THIS RIGHT. NO WORK SHALL BE PERFORMED UNTIL EXPIRATION OF THIS PERIOD.

NOTICE OF CANCELLATION

DATE OF TRANSACTION: _____

YOU MAY CANEL THIS TRANSACTION, WITHOUT ANY PENALTY OR OBLIGATION, WITHIN THREE BUSINESS DAYS FROM THE ABOVE DATE.

IF YOU CANCEL, ANY PROPERTY TRADED IN, ANY PAYMENTS MADE BY YOU UNDER THE CONTRACT OR SALE, AND ANY NEGOTIABLE INSTRUMENT EXECUTED BY YOU WILL BE RETURNED WITHIN TEN BUSINESS DAYS FOLLOWING RECEIPT BY THE SELLER OF YOUR CENCELLATION NOTICE, AND ANY SECURITY INTEREST ARISING OUT OF THE TRANSACTION WILL BE CANCELLED.

IF YOU CANCEL, YOU MUST MAKE AVAILABLE TO THE SELLER AT YOU RESIDENCE, IN SUBSTANTIALLY AS GOOD CONODITION AS WHEN RECEIVED, ANY GOODS DELIVERED TO YOU UNDER THIS CONTRACT OR SALE; OR YOU MAY, IF YOU WISH, COMPLY WITH THE INSTRUCTIONS OF THE SELLER REGARDING THE RETURN SHIPMENT OF THE GOODS AT THE SELLER'S EXPENSE AND RISK.

IF YOU DO MAKE THE GOODS AVAILABLE TO THE SELLER AND THE SELLER DOES NOT PICK THEM UP WITHIN TWNETY DAYS OF THE DATE OF CANCELLATION, YOU MAY RETAIN OR DISPOSE OF THE GOODS WITHOUT ANY FURTHER OBLIGATION. IF YOU FAIL TO MAKE THE GOODS AVAILABLE TO THE SELLER OR IF YOU AGREE TO RETURN THE GOODS TO THE SELLER AND FAIL TO DO SO, THEN YOU REMAIN LIABLE FOR PERFORMANCE OF ALL OBLIGATIONS UNDER THE CONTRACT.

TO CANCEL THIS TRANSACTION, MAIL OR DELIVER
A SIGNED AND DATED COPY OF THIS CANCELLATION
NOTICE OR ANY OTHER WRITTEN NOTICE, OR SEND
A TELEGRAM TO CREATIVE EVOLUTION, LLC AT 227
WHALEHEAD ROAD, GALES FERRY, CONNECTICUT 06335
NOT LATER THAN MIDNIGHT OF _____ .

I HEREBY CANCEL THIS TRANSACTION.

_____   _____
            BUYER   DATE

Basic Supply List

The following is a list of basic supplies you'll need for your decorative painting business. Special jobs may require special equipment, but to start with these things are indispensable.

4' ladder (I prefer the Little Giant)
3" sash paint brush (for latex)
3" paint brush (for latex)
2 sets of roller handles
Roller tray
9" roller covers
3 fabric drop cloths
Box of plastic (to cover furniture)
2" blue painter's tape
Paint can opener
Trash bags
Artist brushes
5-in-one tool
Spackle and trowel (for minor wall repair)
Clean rags
Slim jim with whiz roller covers and tray
Sample boards (I suggest styrene boards)
Kitchen sponges, for clean-up
5 gallon bucket (to carry everything in)
Plastic storage bins, see-through, for storing supplies in your car
    or truck

Quick Reference: Websites

Portfolio: Snapfish www.snapfish.com

Mailing List: InfoUSA www.infousa.com

Credit Card Systems: Merchant Warehouse
www.merchantwarehouse.com

American Society of Interior Decorators: www.asid.org

The Faux Forum: www.fauxforum.com

Learn To Faux: www.learntofaux.com

Instructional DVDs: www.fauxwarehouse.com

Email Newsletters: Constant Contact www.constantcontact.com

To check domain name: www.checkdomain.com

To register domain name: www.dns.com

To verify domain registration information: www.whois.sc

Google Webmaster Guidelines:
www.google.com/support/webmasters/bin/answer.py?answer=35769

Google Webmaster Tools: www.google.com/webmasters/

Matt Cutt's Blog (from Google): www.mattcutts.com/blog

SEO Tools and Opinions:
www.searchenginewatch.com and www.seochat.com

About the Author

Patrick Ganino began his decorative painting career ten years ago with his company, Creative Evolution. He specializes in faux finishes, trompe l'Oeil, and murals. Patrick also developed an online forum for decorative painters at www.fauxforum.com and a site devoted to instructional DVDs from the world's leading decorative painters at www.fauxwarehouse.com. Since 2004, Patrick has taught classes in both decorative painting and business while continuing to run his full-time contracting business. He currently lives in Connecticut with his wife and three children.

Order Form

Check your leading bookstore or order here:

4 Easy ways to order:

ON-LINE: www.fauxwarehouse.com
PHONE: 1-800-345-6665
FAX: (603) 357-2073
Mail: Copy or mail this form to:
        Pathway Book Service
        P.O. Box 89
        #4 Whitebrook Road
        Gilsum, New Hampshire, 03448

YES, I want _____ copies of *The Business of Faux: A Creative Evolution*
at $19.95 plus $3 shipping per book. (VA residents add $1 for state tax) $ _____
* An audio version of this book is also available—to order,
go to: www.fauxwarehouse.com

YES, I want _____copies of *The House that Faux Built:*
Transform Your Home with Paint, Plaster and Creativity.
* Download a free chapter at www.fauxhouse.com).
How-to DVDs are also available.

$34.95 plus $3 shipping per book. (VA residents add $1.50 per book)   + $_____

            Subtract quantity discount, if applicable   - $_____

            Shipping & Handling ($3 per book)   + $_____

            Tax (VA residents Only):   + $_____

                           TOTAL: $_____

Name: _____

Organization: _____

Address: _____

City/State/Zip: _____

Phone: _____   Email: _____

Card Type _____   # _____

Expiration Date:_____   Code: _____

Signature: _____

Quantity Discounts: Order 2-9 copies and subtract 10%. For 10 or more copies, subtract
20%. For larger quantities, contact Pathway Books.